NO ORDINARY BIRD

NO ORDINARY BIRD

Drug Smuggling,
a Plane Crash,
and a Daughter's Quest
for the Truth

ARTIS HENDERSON

HARPER

An Imprint of HarperCollinsPublishers

Without limiting the exclusive rights of any author, contributor or the publisher of this publication, any unauthorized use of this publication to train generative artificial intelligence (AI) technologies is expressly prohibited. HarperCollins also exercise their rights under Article 4(3) of the Digital Single Market Directive 2019/790 and expressly reserve this publication from the text and data mining exception.

NO ORDINARY BIRD. Copyright © 2025 by Artis Henderson. All rights reserved. Printed in the United States of America. No part of this book may be used or reproduced in any manner whatsoever without written permission except in the case of brief quotations embodied in critical articles and reviews. For information, address HarperCollins Publishers, 195 Broadway, New York, NY 10007. In Europe, HarperCollins Publishers, Macken House, 39/40 Mayor Street Upper, Dublin 1, D01 C9W8, Ireland.

HarperCollins books may be purchased for educational, business, or sales promotional use. For information, please email the Special Markets Department at SPsales@harpercollins.com.

hc.com

FIRST EDITION

Designed by Bonni Leon-Berman

Illustration by Meg Palmer Design © Shutterstock

Library of Congress Cataloging-in-Publication Data

Names: Henderson, Artis, author.
Title: No ordinary bird : drug smuggling, a plane crash, and a daughter's quest for the truth / Artis Henderson.
Description: First edition. | New York, NY : Harper, 2025.
Identifiers: LCCN 2024025662 (print) | LCCN 2024025663 (ebook) | ISBN 9780358650270 (hardcover) | ISBN 9780358650287 (ebook)
Subjects: LCSH: Chester, Tilton Lamar, Jr., 1937-1985. | Drug dealers—United States—Biography. | Aircraft accidents—United States.
Classification: LCC HV5805.C5155 H46 2025 (print) | LCC HV5805.C5155 (ebook) | DDC 364.1/3365092—dc23/eng/20250131
LC record available at https://lccn.loc.gov/2024025662
LC ebook record available at https://lccn.loc.gov/2024025663

25 26 27 28 29 LBC 5 4 3 2 1

For my family, lost and found.

> But Jonathan Livingston Seagull, unashamed, stretching his wings again in that trembling hard curve—slowing, slowing, and stalling once more—was no ordinary bird.
>
> —RICHARD BACH, *JONATHAN LIVINGSTON SEAGULL*

Contents

Author's Note ... ix

Prologue: The Accident ... 1

PART I

1. Wrightsville ... 7
2. No Ordinary Bird ... 12
3. Family Man ... 19
4. Lamar and Artis ... 24

PART II

5. First Run ... 35
6. The Transportation Guy ... 47
7. Monopoly Money ... 53
8. "That's Not Chicken Feed, but It Will Buy a Lot of It!" ... 58
9. Bill, Terry, and Jen ... 66
10. The Islands ... 76
11. Operation Lone Star ... 83
12. Welcome to the World, Baby Girl ... 89

PART III

13. The Drug Problem ... 95
14. The Lesley Bickerton Affair ... 100
15. Darby ... 108
16. The Indictment ... 116
17. The Bahamian Royal Commission of Inquiry ... 120

18	The Arrest	132
19	WITSEC	138
20	The Courthouse	140
21	Summer 1985	148

PART IV

22	Disappeared	153
23	Uncle Tony	163
24	Covert Agent	170
25	The Woodwork	186
26	Ron Elliott	190
27	Homecoming	194
28	The Field	213
29	Redmond Wells	218
30	Family	220

Acknowledgments   227

Author's Note

This is a work of nonfiction. It is the product of extensive interviews and primary-source investigation. Most of the dialogue is taken from newspaper articles and court transcripts. Some is re-created based on the memory of those present. The following is a list of pseudonyms used in the book: Salvador (Sal), Corinne, Frog, Leonard, Durbin McCollum, Ethan McCollum, Milton Percy, Blue Hollow Retreat, Victor Obert, and Redmond Wells. Though I've put thousands of hours of research into this book, it's still told from my own unique viewpoint. I'm grappling with this story as much as I'm reporting it.

NO ORDINARY BIRD

Prologue

The Accident

June 20, 1985

I REMEMBER THE PLANE, A single-engine Piper Cub. It was white with a red stripe running down the side. I remember my father in the pilot's seat. I remember the late afternoon humming with a yellow heat. We were on our farm in North Georgia, five hundred acres at the foothills of the Blue Ridge Mountains. I had just turned five years old. My dad was forty-seven. He'd spent the day baling hay, and there were still straws of it stuck in his hair.

My mother stood at the open door of the plane. Her hair was long and dark and parted in the middle. She had it tied back in a loose knot. Though she was forty, she could have passed for a woman ten years younger. She was barefoot, wearing a pair of cutoffs and a T-shirt, trailed by the stray pups that had made their way to our farm. Her face was bare of makeup, and she had an easy, natural beauty. Most days she came flying with us, and I'd sit on her lap. But on this day she was too busy. Instead of coming, she tightened the seat belt until it bit into my skin.

"Ow," I said.

She tightened it harder.

The airplane was a two-seater with the seats set in tandem, one behind the other. I could see my dad over the back of his seat. He wore a pair of aviator sunglasses and a headset.

"You sure you don't want to come?" he asked my mom again.

She shook her head and closed the plane door. "I've got too much to do."

My dad looked at me over his shoulder. "You ready, A.J.?"

I beamed up at him. Though my dad had three living children from a previous marriage, they were already grown. I was his late-in-life baby, the only child my father and mother had together. We flew almost every day for the pure fun of it, the simple pleasure of moving through the air. I knew the routines, the way my dad cranked the engine and the propeller turned. The way he taxied to the grass runway. How he pulled on the yoke as we picked up speed and lifted into the air. That afternoon, we rose over the farm and banked so that I could see the wooded expanse of the land below. The dogwoods and daffodils had already bloomed, and the surrounding forest was settling into a mountain summer. We flew over oaks and maples thick with greenery. A creek ran near the house, a cold stream of clear water where salamanders hid beneath flat stones. My father's herd of cattle stood in the open pasture, looking skyward as we buzzed overhead. The metal roofs on his chicken houses glinted in the late afternoon sun. I looked down on blueberry bushes and rows of muscadine grapes. This was our farm, our home, our acreage, and I took unquestioning joy in its sun-dappled beauty.

My dad flew over the guesthouse where my mom's parents, my grandparents Art and Jewel, were staying that summer. They came out onto the porch and waved. He circled above them so I could wave down. Then he turned to head back to the runway. It was only a quarter mile away.

Later, my grandpa said that's when the plane jerked unnaturally. Maybe that's why I sat forward. I don't know. The emptiness in my memory where that moment should be has haunted me all my life. What I do remember is leaning close to the back of my father's seat and asking, "Daddy, are we going to crash?"

"No, baby," he said to me. "Sit back down."

He pointed the plane toward a clearing in the trees. But before the Piper Cub could reach the open space, it fell out of the sky. We went into the ground nose-first, and the plane toppled upside down in the red Georgia clay. My grandparents were watching, horrified, from the deck of their house. They rushed to the clearing, where the plane lay crumpled on the ground. My grandpa said later that he smelled gas, gas everywhere, and he was certain the plane would catch fire. That's why he pulled me free. He looked to my father in the front seat, but my dad was already dead.

Authorities were on the scene quickly. Too quickly, some say. There were agents from the Georgia Bureau of Investigation, the local sheriff's office, and the Federal Aviation Administration. A reporter overheard them talking and printed their conversation in the newspaper the next day. "I guess the prosecutors down in Atlanta will be drinking double Scotches and dancing in the streets tonight," one of them said.

I SPENT THE first three days after the plane crash in a coma with a fractured skull and a broken vertebra. The doctors said my chances of surviving were low. Everybody held their breath and waited. Finally, my dad's attorney announced to reporters, "The baby looks like she's going to make it." By then, everyone had a name for the crash. They called it *the accident*.

Four days after the accident, while I was still at the hospital, a memorial service was held for my father at a funeral home in Cleveland, Georgia. His casket—closed—was covered with roses. My mother stood beside it. When a reporter who had written about my father's case paid his respects, she told him, sobbing, "This isn't the way it was supposed to end."

The service, in many ways, mirrored what my father's trial for drug smuggling might have looked like that summer if he had survived to attend it. His lead defense attorney spoke. His best friend spoke. His oldest son, my half brother Bill, spoke. My father's brother, my uncle Tony, would have liked to have spoken, but he wasn't cleared to attend the service. Tony was already in the federal witness protection program by then.

Those who spoke called my dad by different names. Some called him Lamar, his middle name, which is what my mom and most of his friends called him. Some called him Junie, his growing-up name, because he was Tilton Lamar Chester Jr. No one used the name they called him in Colombia, Sin Sueño, a name that my father proudly translated as "One Who Never Sleeps." Instead, they talked about my father as a hero. They said he was generous, intelligent, charismatic, patriotic. "He was a man of class and style in a time when there is very little class and style," his attorney said. My dad's best friend called him an eternal optimist. "Lamar wasn't afraid of death," he said. "His only fear was that he might not live life to its fullest."

Everybody said the same thing. My dad was a good guy. But in all of the eulogies, no one mentioned my father's favorite expression, a line he had repeated often to the many reporters who always seemed to be at our house.

You can't tell the good guys from the bad guys.

PART I

1

Wrightsville

MY FATHER, TILTON LAMAR CHESTER Jr., was born in Atlanta, Georgia, in 1937. His family lived in Wrightsville, a rural town in central Georgia most famous for being on the path of William Tecumseh Sherman's March to the Sea. In the larger world of 1937, Europe was bracing itself for another war. Amelia Earhart disappeared over the Pacific. The *Hindenburg* caught fire. Dust storms continued to decimate the American plains. Franklin D. Roosevelt was inaugurated for a second term. A gallon of gas cost ten cents.

For most people in rural Georgia, including my father, poverty was the rule. The Great Depression would have a hold on the country until the United States entered World War II, and conditions were especially bleak in the South, even for landowners. On the outskirts of Wrightsville, Lamar's grandma, Ma Dell, lived on a hundred acres. Her father had been the town doctor, which was how she came by her land. After she divorced her husband, she moved back to the land and the house she grew up in, an unpainted wood structure with a tin roof and a front porch but no indoor plumbing or electricity. Ma Dell rented out her fields for growing cotton and hay, but in the time between the wars, even with all that land, she was still poor.

My dad and his family would move around a lot during his

early years, but he always came back to Ma Dell's in the summer. He was a skinny kid with a crew cut, wearing patched-up clothes, barefoot because he only owned one pair of shoes and he needed to save them for winter. Already, the feeling of not having enough—and not being enough—smoldered within him. Those summers at Ma Dell's left an impression on my father that he would carry for the rest of his life. Georgia sank into his soul, and he spent years yearning to get back. I imagine him in the early morning sitting on the front porch of Ma Dell's, his bare feet propped on the rails, watching the fog roll in across the fields. My father didn't believe in religion, though he wasn't an atheist. He believed in fate. In that moment, he couldn't have known what fate had written for him—wealth and power and the eventual loss of all of it—but what he could see were the alternatives: scarcity and hardship. I like to believe this is the moment my father looked out over the fog-covered pasture and set a goal for himself. One day he would be a rich man, he decided, and he would own land in the state of Georgia. More than Ma Dell's hundred acres. A parcel where all the land he could see belonged to him.

LAMAR'S MAMA, LOUISE, was known for her temper. She beat her boys with a switch in the front yard. She beat her daughter with a shoe. Behind her back, her children called her Lou-fucking-uise. My dad's pop, Tilton Lamar Chester Sr., had come to North Georgia with the Civilian Conservation Corps, part of FDR's New Deal. The Conservation Corps put young men to work restoring parks and forests. After his stint in the corps, Pop became a carpenter, though he had trouble keeping a job. Part of it was his drinking and part of it was the fact that no one in my family takes orders well. Tell us what to do, and we'll just as soon tell you to go fuck yourself. That bad attitude combined with a stiff drink meant that Pop was often out of work.

There's a photo of Pop taken when he was a young man, dressed in work coveralls and sitting astride an Indian motorcycle. He's got the wide Chester grin and the proud Chester brow, and he shines with an unmistakable virility. Pop would have four wives in his lifetime. Some say he had many mistresses. In this particular photo, Pop is broad-shouldered and confident. Not cocky, that cheap and flimsy stance, but sure of himself. He was a man who could fix things, who was at ease with a hammer and a hacksaw. He could take apart a truck engine and raise a barn in the same day. He wasn't wealthy or educated, and in many power structures he would have been a powerless man. But in rural Georgia in the first decades of the twentieth century, he was a force.

After the end of World War II, when my father was in his early teens, the family settled in Coral Springs, just outside Miami. The booming Florida construction industry needed workers, and Pop found a job. By now, there were four Chester children—Lamar, Judy, Jerry, and Tony. Pop raised them with a firm understanding that *can't* wasn't part of their vocabulary. "I don't ever want to hear you say you can't do anything," he'd tell them.

As the firstborn, Lamar was endowed with the natural leadership qualities of many firstborns. He became an Eagle Scout and he excelled at fishing, camping, and pranking. He was the leader of his pack of rowdy teenage boys. Every now and then they liked to stick potatoes in the tailpipes of police cars. When the cars started, the potatoes would explode out of the pipe with a loud bang. The boys would laugh and laugh.

In 1957 Lamar got hitched to a local girl named Nancy. Nancy was just sixteen and worried about getting pregnant. That's why they drove from Miami to the courthouse in Wrightsville, where my dad's aunt arranged a quick wedding. The plan was to keep the marriage a secret. Nancy would live at home and finish high school, and then they'd have a proper ceremony. But one of Nancy's sisters told their father, and by the time Nancy got home, she'd been kicked out. Which is how my freewheeling, fun-loving father found himself supporting a wife at nineteen. Nancy's plans to finish high school also went out the door. Married girls weren't allowed to attend. It's hard to ignore the irony of what came next. Nancy had gotten married to avoid the social risks of getting pregnant too early, but as soon as she got married, getting pregnant seemed like the only option left to her. So she set about having babies. Their first, Bill, arrived a year after the wedding. Soon they had two more, both boys, Terry and Richard. These would be my brothers.

Lamar did what he could to support Nancy and the boys. He drove a taxi. He started a plant nursery. He taught himself to scuba dive and worked for the local golf courses, retrieving lost balls from the water hazards. He'd scrub off the grass stains and sell the extras to the rich guys playing the greens. He was always working, striving, pushing to move up.

By this time he'd adopted the look that would carry him into the 1970s, a crew cut styled with a dollop of Brylcreem and a clean-shaven face splashed with English Leather. He'd grown to his full height, six-foot-three, and he'd stayed skinny. He had the wide Chester forehead and the smooth Chester grin, but on his face he also had the Chester acne—terrible, scarring, cystic acne that runs in our family. It does a strange thing to a person to have the most visible part of your body affected in this way. I know from personal experience. I've had terrible skin since I was thirteen. It's hard for me to talk about it, even here. I've tried everything—dermatologists, endocrinologists, allergists, nutritionists, acupuncturists, chiropractors, Reiki masters, and faith healers—but no one has been able to fix it. I can't say what it was like for my dad, but I can tell you what it's been like for me. I have a deep conviction of being flawed. My whole life I wanted to be beautiful, but when I look in the mirror I see a monster. Perhaps my father felt that way, too. Maybe it underlay many of his decisions.

Eventually my dad did what many young men of limited means do—he joined the armed services, first the navy and then the air force. In the air force he earned his aircraft mechanic's license and started a side business fixing wrecked aircraft, keeping broken-down planes in the yard beside the house. He was nuts about planes. He liked their mechanical precision and the technical challenge of flying them, and he enjoyed the sense of freedom that came with being in the air. And he wasn't the only one. By this time, aviation had become a national obsession. From the first flight of the Wright brothers in 1903 to Charles Lindbergh's nonstop solo flight between New York and Paris in 1927 to the bombers of World War II and the introduction of commercial aircraft in the 1950s, Americans were obsessed with flying. After his stint in the air force, my dad got his private pilot's license and was hired on with a small freight carrier. His brother Tony was also working around airplanes as a stock clerk. The day my dad took Tony up in a four-seat, single-engine, retractable-gear 1949 Navion was the day that Tony knew he wanted to be a pilot too. Lamar let him take the controls, and Tony was hooked. Flying had officially entered the Chester family.

2

No Ordinary Bird

IN 1969 MY FATHER WAS hired as a pilot for Eastern Airlines, a big national carrier based out of Miami. Though he flew professionally, he would have flown just as much if he weren't getting a paycheck. He liked what most pilots like about flying—a sense of weightlessness, the thrill of traveling above the earth, the adrenaline bump that comes with controlled but dangerous activities. But my dad didn't just want to be a good pilot. He wanted to be an exceptional pilot. That drive toward exceptionalism had an element of testing the limits of what was safe. He liked flying at its rawest and most dangerous. He once made a bet that he could land a plane on the sideways axis of a runway. He did. I'm tempted to use the word *reckless* to describe him, but that's not accurate. My father was calculated. In everything he did, he was very much in control. If he made decisions that most sane people would call dangerous, it was because he'd carefully considered them. I wish I could tell you that I grew up to be wary of this type of person, but to this day there's something terribly compelling to me about the idea of a brilliant man skating on the edge of disaster.

Around this time, Richard Bach's *Jonathan Livingston Seagull* was published. First printed serially in *Flying* magazine in the late 1960s, *Jonathan Livingston Seagull* went on to top the *New York*

Times bestseller list for thirty-seven weeks. It was my father's favorite book. I don't know a pilot from those days who doesn't own a copy. The story is a fable, of sorts, about a seagull who pushes the boundaries of flight. It has insider flying references that pilots geek out on, like talk of altitude and windspeed, glides and stalls. It also relays an underlying message that appeals to the kind of person who likes to fly: life is about more than the daily squabble. I've read and reread *Jonathan Livingston Seagull*, looking for clues about my father in its pages. This passage stands out:

> But way off alone, out by himself beyond boat and shore, Jonathan Livingston Seagull was practicing. A hundred feet in the sky he lowered his webbed feet, lifted his beak, and strained to hold a painful hard twisting curve through his wings. The curve meant that he would fly slowly, and now he slowed until the wind was a whisper in his face, until the ocean stood still beneath him. He narrowed his eyes in fierce concentration, held his breath, forced one . . . single . . . more . . . inch . . . of . . . curve. . . . Then his feathers ruffled, he stalled and fell.
>
> Seagulls, as you know, never falter, never stall. To stall in the air is for them disgrace and dishonor.
>
> But Jonathan Livingston Seagull, unashamed, stretching his wings again in that trembling hard curve—slowing, slowing, and stalling once more—was no ordinary bird.

Those words—*no ordinary bird*—capture my dad's approach to flying perfectly. Though he wouldn't take risks in the cockpit of a commercial airplane, he was known for taking risks in his own planes. These risks usually panned out, like the time he flew from Miami to Georgia and landed with less than five minutes of flying time's worth of gas. His brother Tony refueled the plane and joked that there was only half a gallon left in the tank. After that, my dad had a new nickname—Point-Five.

But his risks didn't always pan out.

Like the time he ferried Pop and Pop's third wife, Vera, from Georgia to Florida. Tony came with them to the airport to fuel up the plane and see them off. Before they left, Tony took Pop aside. "Make sure Junie stops for gas no farther south than Vero Beach," Tony said.

My dad and his parents took off late in the day. They were flying in Lamar's single-engine Cessna 206. The 206 is a workhorse, often used as a bush plane in remote areas. As the plane traveled south, the sun set and the moon rose in the night sky. Lamar never stopped for gas. Pilots tell me there is always an element of fear in flying. There has to be. There are too many moving parts and too many opportunities for mechanical failure—there's too much distance between the plane and the ground—not to be afraid. On this flight my father would have seen the danger coming, minute by minute, as the gauge on the fuel tank dropped toward zero. He would have known that flying from western Georgia to southern Florida on a single tank of gas was risky. I imagine that his twin demons of exceptionalism and overconfidence warred against the saner parts of his nature, the parts that said he should have stopped to refuel hours ago.

But like Jonathan Livingston Seagull, my dad wanted to push the limits of flight to its outermost edges. When my brothers were learning to fly as teenagers, our father liked to do an exercise with them. He would kill the engine while they were in midair. "Now look around," he'd say to the boy at the controls. "Where are you going to land?" It was an instinct he wanted to teach them early—always have a landing spot in mind.

I like to think my dad had a landing spot in mind when, ten

miles from the Opa-locka airport, the engine of the Cessna 206 quit. It was too early for him to have started his landing approach, and the plane would have been at five thousand to six thousand feet. That's about a mile. A mile above the ground. When a plane runs out of gas, it's similar to a car running out of gas. There's a sputtering, a choking, and then a coasting. When a car runs out of gas, there's an immediate silence as the engine noises die off. When a plane runs out of gas, the engine noises stop, but there's still the sound of wind rushing past the airframe.

I play this story out in my mind, and my father is cool and collected. He handles the controls with ease. He knows just what to do. But in reality, he would have been scared. The noise of the wind outside the plane, without the roar of the engine, would have been unfamiliar and frightening. Though a small-engine aircraft slips into a glide when its engine quits, that glide can feel erratic. In the first moments the plane drops quickly, a thousand feet in the five seconds it takes to figure out what's happening. I imagine that my father's stomach lurched, and cold adrenaline shot up the back of his neck.

Or maybe I'm not imagining. Perhaps I'm remembering. Not from this crash but from the other one, the one that killed him and almost killed me. Maybe it's not my father's fear I'm thinking about, but my own.

High above the Everglades, my father would have been looking for a place to land. Maybe he was looking even before the plane ran out of gas. Maybe he was always looking. On this night, he got lucky. It was early fall, the beginning of the dry season in South Florida, and by the light of the moon he was able to spot a flat piece of dirt. The landing had to be timed perfectly. There was no room for error. The Cessna 206 is a tripod plane with two wheels in the back and one in the front. If the nose came down on soft ground or tall grass while the plane was still moving at high speed, then it would flip.

I see it clearly. A patch of dry earth cast in silvered moonlight. The plane dropping toward the ground. My father at the controls, pulling back on the throttle as the wheels touched the earth. He tipped the left wing down as the plane landed, purposefully sending it into a ground loop and circling, preventing it from flipping. There was substantial damage to the left wing but nowhere else. Vera broke her wrist, but both Lamar and Pop were unhurt.

The air traffic controllers at Opa-locka had watched the lights on the plane descend into the Everglades. They sent out a rescue team. The next day, the National Transportation Safety Board performed a formal investigation. The NTSB investigates all crashes that happen within the United States, both commercial and private, whether or not there are casualties. The investigators on this crash labeled the type of accident "engine failure or malfunction." For probable causes, they listed "pilot in command—mismanagement of fuel" and "miscalculated fuel consumption; fuel exhaustion." Put simply, the plane had run out of gas.

Eventually, the 206 came back to the house in Cutler Ridge on a flatbed trailer. This is standard practice after a crash. Once the NTSB has performed its investigation, the airplane is returned to its owner. My dad would spend the next few weeks in the side yard working with sheet metal, fixing the damage to the wing. Later, the Cessna 206 would become part of his drug smuggling operation. He named it the Hulk, because it could take a beating.

WITHIN MY DAD'S family, people tell the story of the Everglades crash often. It's told with a kind of reverence, and the moral is usually the same—what an excellent pilot he was, how he managed to land the plane at night in a wild stretch of dirt and sawgrass, nobody hurt except for Vera and her broken wrist. He was just ten miles from Opa-locka, they say. The tower could see his lights. He almost made it.

But it's worth noting that Pop and Vera didn't participate in this mythmaking. To them, it wasn't a heroic story, a tale of grit and valor. It was a dangerous, avoidable mistake. Afterward, Pop sued Lamar over the crash. Although the case never went anywhere, hard feelings clearly lingered long after the incident had entered family lore.

The Everglades crash was a sobering experience for my father. I'd like to believe he learned a valuable lesson about pushing an aircraft to its limits. He never ran out of fuel again. Unless we're counting the crash that killed him.

BY NOW, MY dad and Nancy's three sons were little boys. Bill, the firstborn, was extremely bright, a dark-haired child with thick glasses and a shy laugh. Terry was whip-smart and quick-grinned, a peacemaker and popular. Richard was the baby, a sweet-faced cherub that everyone doted on. The boys were loved equally. Much later, as adults, they'll agree that there was no hint of favoritism when they were children.

Their childhood was like something out of *Tom Sawyer*—outdoorsy, active, barefoot. They spent their days shooting slingshots, building fires, climbing trees. Lamar raised his boys with the same words he'd been taught by his pop: *can't* wasn't in the Chester vocabulary. "Don't ever tell me you can't do anything," he'd say. The boys would nod and study their father carefully. They spent long afternoons watching him fix the planes he kept in the side yard. Lamar pressed his lips together as he concentrated, pursing them in the middle like he might suck on a straw, while the boys waited eagerly, ready to pass over tools, worried that their father might ask for a screwdriver and they'd hand him a wrench. They hated to let him down. Not that Lamar got angry with his boys. He never yelled. He didn't threaten. The only time they heard him cuss was when he was working on a broken plane. "It just doesn't work until you cuss at it," he liked to say.

I recently found a black-and-white studio portrait of my dad's first family taken during this time. In it my father is dressed in a dark blazer and slim black tie, a white pocket square folded neatly in his breast pocket. His hair is shaved into a tight crew cut. Nancy sits beside him in a long-sleeved black dress buttoned to her neck. She wears a string of pearls and has short hair and a tight-lipped smile. Bill and Terry stand behind them, still small, dressed in dark jackets and slim ties like their father. Their little-boy ears stick out from the sides of their heads, set off by crew cuts. Richard is a baby in my father's lap. Everyone except my father looks to the right, under the direction of the photographer. They smile a version of their school-portrait smiles, all mouth and no eyes. Only my dad looks directly into the camera, his eyes crinkling at the corners, grinning a devil-may-care grin. It's as if he sees something that the others don't see, a future on the horizon that no one but him can imagine.

3

Family Man

THE UNITED STATES HAD FULLY embraced the jet-set age, and being a commercial airline pilot carried a certain glamour. The uniform helped; my father looked dashing in his black suit with the gold bars on his shoulders. So did the salary. In his first year with Eastern he made $30,000, enough to propel them into the middle class. The family bought a three-bedroom ranch house in Cutler Ridge, a suburb of Miami. The roof was flat, and Lamar climbed up on it with his boys to watch the Apollo launch. The interior had shag carpeting, terrazzo floors, and rattan furniture. Lamar built a wall of shelving and filled it with his albums—Herb Alpert & the Tijuana Brass, Engelbert Humperdinck, Harry Belafonte. He kept his monthly subscriptions to *Popular Mechanics*, *Flying*, and *Playboy* in a magazine rack beside the couch. He didn't own many books. Other than *Jonathan Livingston Seagull*, he wasn't a reader. But he did love chess. A cheap plastic chess set from the drugstore lived on the game shelf beside Parcheesi and Twister.

Lamar and Nancy were a social couple, and their house in Cutler Ridge became the place for parties. Through a haze of cigarette smoke, people danced to Motown from a record player in the corner. They drank gin and tonics and tall glasses of yellow Galliano. The women wore sleeveless shifts in pale pastels. The men dressed in narrow slacks and short-sleeved shirts. They grouped together outside and clinked the ice in their glasses as they talked. Lamar liked to tell airline pilot jokes. His favorite one was about three friends—an architect, a doctor, and a pilot—who each had a golden retriever. One day, the three friends took the dogs hunting to find out which retriever was the best. The architect shot a duck first.

"Go get it, girl," he said to his retriever.

The retriever swam out to the duck, drew a quick set of blueprints, built an ark, and sailed the duck back to her master.

"Pretty good," the two other friends said.

Next, the doctor spotted a duck and shot it.

"Go get it, girl," he said to his retriever.

The dog swam out to the duck, defeathered it, made a neat incision along the belly, gutted it, sutured it, then brought the duck back to her master.

"Pretty good," the two other friends said.

Finally, the airline pilot shot a duck.

"Go get it, boy," he commanded his retriever.

The dog leaped into the lake, swam out to the duck, ate the duck, swam back, fucked the other two dogs, and then took ten days off.

Jesus, I think.

This was the tone of my father's world, the kind of atmosphere that backyard barbecues and cocktail parties were steeped in. What made a "good" man in those days was so dramatically different from what makes a "good" man today that I sometimes have a hard time wrapping my head around this person who was smart and funny and charismatic and also—let's be honest—thriving in a world of toxic masculinity.

I often wonder whether Nancy was happy married to my father.

She passed away in 2012, so I can't ask her myself. But people tell me that she, too, was funny and smart, a writer with ambitions to write a book herself. Her mother was French, which gave her a certain worldliness in a part of Florida where that was rare. She had a wide group of friends. She smoked Virginia Slims because they were the feminist cigarette. She didn't mind my dad's dirty jokes. Their neighborhood in Cutler Ridge was full of pilots, and she was used to their bawdy humor. And anyway, she was a jokester herself. Once in the house in Cutler Ridge, on a cool afternoon when one of her sisters was visiting, she got it in her head to light the gas fireplace—which she'd never tried before. By the time she held the match to the fumes, the gas had been running for a while. It ignited with a flash that blackened her face and singed off her eyebrows. She turned around to look at her sister, who stood there gaping, and joked, "Do you mind if I smoke?"

Nancy had three children before she was twenty, which didn't leave much time for her own ambitions. I know there was strain on the marriage early—the everyday strain of young children and the very real weight of making ends meet. But my father's relationships with other women were also a stressor.

On first pass, people tell me my father was brilliant and magnetic. But on second pass, or if they've had a few drinks, they'll admit that he had other qualities, the shadow side of those appealing traits. Though he was extremely charming, my father often used that charm as a launching point for affairs with women. He had learned from his father that being a "real man" was important. Maybe the most important thing of all. And his definition of a "real man" was someone who had women on their side.

Yet even though his extramarital affairs certainly contributed to the end of his relationship with Nancy, they weren't what ultimately destroyed his marriage. It was grief.

By the time their third son, Richard, had his first birthday, Lamar and Nancy noticed that something was wrong. Richard had begun to show signs of early developmental delays. His head grew large while his body stayed small. The features of his face took on strange proportions. Eventually, doctors concluded that Richard had Hurler syndrome, a rare genetic disorder that causes dwarfism and severe facial misconfiguration. There's another name for Hurler that has mercifully fallen out of favor: gargoylism. Most children with Hurler don't survive past ten.

The family's orbit came to center around Richard. He was sweet and liked being tickled. He'd tell anyone who tried to call him Ricky that he was "Richard, not Ricky." He was a whiz at the card game Memory; nobody could beat him. Lamar doted on his youngest son. With Richard, he brought all his gentleness to bear. He taught his two oldest boys to be Richard's defenders, and the boys looked out for their little brother. They didn't truck with anyone who used the word *retard*. As soon as they were old enough, each of the boys joined the Boy Scouts, including Richard. Lamar was there for fishing trips and overnight camping. He tied knots. He whittled wood. He told scary stories around the campfire, Richard by his side. When Richard got a little older, Lamar took the kids from his special needs school flying. They each got to sit in the front seat of the plane and hold the yoke in their hands.

I often forget that Richard was my half brother. He would have had to live another decade for us to be alive on the planet at the same time and another decade after that to have cemented in my memory. As it is, he feels as distant and unattached to me as long-dead great-grandparents. But still he was my brother, as closely related to me as my other half siblings. I'd heard about Richard growing up, though not in great detail, and mostly in the context of my own creation story. My mom had demanded an amniocentesis when she was pregnant with me, though the procedure was still new and relatively untested. She and my father were worried about the possibility of having another child with Hurler. They both knew, in their own way, that their hearts couldn't handle it.

As Richard neared his tenth birthday, he became increasingly susceptible to infections. His small, malformed body grew weaker and weaker. One night he went into the hospital with pneumonia. Our father sat with him for hours, but eventually the nurses insisted he go home and get some rest. Richard died during the night, when no one was there. I think my dad carried that burden for the rest of his life.

Richard was buried in his Boy Scout uniform. At the funeral, our father cried in great heaving sobs. He didn't try to wipe away the tears that ran down his cheeks. It was the only time his boys had seen him cry.

For my other two brothers, Richard's death marked the end of their childhood. At night, they'd lie in their bunk beds and speculate about where Richard had gone, to heaven or if he existed in some other form. Their brother's absence left a hole in the family that was impossible to fill.

Grief is hard on any marriage, and my father's first marriage, with trouble already brewing under the surface, wasn't destined to survive. Still, in the perplexing duality of life where sadness and joy are forever intertwined, Nancy discovered that she was pregnant soon after Richard died. This would be her fourth baby, my sister Jennifer, born in 1971. But by the time Jen arrived, our father was already on his way out.

4

Lamar and Artis

PEOPLE TELL ME THERE WERE two Lamars: the Lamar before my mother, Artis, and the Lamar after. The Lamar before Artis kept his hair short. He listened to Merle Haggard and Waylon Jennings. He was pro-Vietnam, and he never smoked marijuana. The Lamar after Artis listened to Marvin Gaye. He wore bell bottoms. He let his hair grow past the tops of his ears. He had a mustache. He still wasn't crazy about marijuana, but he was willing to give it a try.

This change might have been my mother's influence, but more than anything it was a product of the times. My father had been born at the tail end of the Great Depression. He was alive for World War II, though too young to fight, and he came of age in the 1950s. The soundtrack of his youth was sung by crooners like Nat King Cole and Frank Sinatra. The rock and roll of Elvis Presley didn't burst onto the scene until he was nineteen. Popular TV shows like *Leave It to Beaver* were still in black and white.

If my dad's youth was spent in the Brylcreemed decade of postwar optimism, then his early adulthood was rocked by the forces of the 1960s. Change swirled around him. He was twenty-six when the Beatles topped the charts with their first album, and almost twenty-seven when Kennedy was assassinated. He was thirty-one when the tide turned on Vietnam. He lived through a decade that saw the civil rights movement and the first man on the moon. *Leave It to Beaver* was out, and forward-facing shows like *Lost in Space* were in. Times were changing, and my dad couldn't help but change with them.

My mother, Artis, was seven years younger than Lamar, and from an entire other generation. The year the Beatles went to number one, Lamar was already married, with three young children and a station wagon in his driveway. Artis was just graduating from high school. She was a freshman in college when JFK was shot. She was engaged to her first husband, but not yet married, when Neil Armstrong walked on the moon. She'd rolled her hair in orange juice cans at night when she was a teenager, trying to get Jackie Kennedy's perfect flip, but by the late 1960s she was wearing her dark hair parted in the middle and hanging to her waist, like Cher. She stacked her wrists with silver bracelets and slid turquoise rings on her fingers. She wasn't afraid to wear miniskirts.

In fact, she wasn't afraid of much. My mom grew up on a farm in central Florida, near the banks of Lake Okeechobee. She was raised in the sugarcane town of Clewiston, where she developed a rugged toughness early. On weekend mornings, she'd grab the horse grazing in their pasture and set off riding bareback across the citrus groves and cattle ranches that ringed their property. The horse would try to unseat her with low-hanging branches, but my mom would just hold on tighter, whooping. When the local bully threatened to beat up her little brother, my mom punched the bully in the face. He gave her a wide berth after that. Not surprisingly, my mom had a hard mouth and liked to cuss. But she was also funny, and she had the added benefit of being pretty. Her toughness, her sense of humor, and her looks combined to make her the kind of girl people wanted to be around. In high school, she was voted most popular.

By all accounts, her parents had a happy marriage. Her father, Art, was the postmaster. Her mother, Jewel, delivered mail. They were kind, hardworking people in the old tradition. Their families had been early settlers in Florida. They went to the Presbyterian church in town every Sunday. They didn't swear or drink, but they weren't holy rollers either. On vacation, they liked to tow an Airstream around the state. Art grew gardenias in the front yard and brought Jewel one every morning. Jewel collected French perfume and tubes of rouge and pretty high heels that she wore on her small feet. Though everyone in town called her Miss Jewel, Art called her Frenchie. The story went that when she was in high school, she appeared in a play dressed as a French maid. Nothing provocative, of course. Art, who was sitting in the audience, sat forward. "Who's that?" he asked the friend next to him. "Jewel Lowe," the friend said. Art nodded and watched the pretty girl onstage. "I'm going to marry her," he said.

My mom went to college at the University of Miami, where she quickly met a man named Salvador who came from a wealthy New York family. In my conversations with Sal for this book, he was polite and kind. He spoke of my mom fondly and still remembered her birthday. But in the 1960s Sal was young and brash. That brashness would later make him a wildly successful businessman, but it didn't necessarily make him a great life partner at that moment. My mom and Sal were married in 1969 at the Church of the Little Flower in Coral Gables. She wore a floor-length white gown with long sleeves and handmade lace stitched at her wrists. She had four bridesmaids dressed in pink. The groomsmen wore tuxedos.

What stands out to me from the wedding photos is that Sal is not smiling in any of them, not when he's walking down the aisle or sitting in the back of the limo or moving stiffly on the dance floor. He's not smiling as he feeds his new wife cake. In the moments when they might have held hands, my mom's hand is looped through his arm instead. His hands hang at his sides.

Unlike Sal, my mom is smiling in all of the photos, a wide smile with lifted brows and a look that seems to say, "Am I doing this right?" I recognize that look. I do it too, especially when I'm nervous. Or when I'm uncertain. But my mom wasn't uncertain—those who cared about her were. Before she'd walked down the aisle in her elaborate white dress, she'd stood with her father inside the church vestibule, listening for the organ to cue the wedding march. That's when her dad—my gentle-hearted grandpa Art—reached into the pocket of his suit pants and pulled out his car keys. He knew what a loving, happy marriage looked like, and he recognized that this was not destined to be that kind. He put the keys in my mom's hand.

"Take the car and go," he said. "No one will blame you."

This was a radical moment. Women had enormous pressure to make a good match and marry early. My mom was doing just that. She was twenty-four and marrying a man on the rise. My grandpa's willingness to help her back out—at the last moment, after the enormous expense of the wedding—is a testament to how deeply he cared for his daughter.

My mom looked down at the keys in her hand. She loved Sal. That was true. She also wanted a life bigger than what she'd had growing up beside the Okeechobee. She didn't know in that moment that she'd come to need more than Sal could give her. He was offering her a good life, and a good life felt like enough. She held the keys for just a beat before passing them back. When the organ music started, she walked down the aisle and married Sal.

BUT GRANDPA ART was right. By 1971, just two years later, the marriage was already on the rocks. Sal wasn't abusive. He wasn't cruel. They simply weren't a good fit.

And my mom was no wilting flower. At this point, she was teaching at one of the roughest high schools in Dade County. Among her students and colleagues, she was known as a strong teacher—fair, good in the classroom, but not to be messed with.

My mom's girlfriends knew she wasn't happy in her marriage, and one of them—who happened to be dating an Eastern Airlines pilot—suggested setting my mom up with another pilot.

"We'll all have drinks together," the friend said. "It'll be fun."

My mom wasn't sure. Even on the heels of the sexual revolution of the 1960s, her roots ran deep in conservative Florida. It was hard to shake her rural values. But her own situation with Sal wasn't making her happy. And anyway, she reasoned, it was just drinks with friends, not a *date*.

She was introduced to Lamar at the friend's apartment later that week. He looked dashing in his Eastern Airlines uniform, just back from a round-trip flight to Puerto Rico. He brought her a pineapple he'd picked up that morning in San Juan.

"Anyone can bring flowers," he said, smiling with the full force of his flirtatious charm.

The chemistry between them was immediate. It would take a brave man to court my mother, partly because she was intimidating and partly because she was Sal's wife. Sal had everything my father didn't: a good family, a good education, and a good future ahead of him. What my father had was boldness, and he pursued my mom with all the forthright intention, the humor and delight, that would come to define their relationship. Never mind the fact that both of them were still married.

THIS WAS MY mom's first affair, but it was not my father's. True to form, he'd had a steady stream of women on the side throughout his marriage to Nancy. They came and went, barely leaving any wake. But my mother was different. Artis was special, people tell me. She was self-possessed and sophisticated in her ideas. She was, in truth, out of my father's league. He knew it, and it created a schoolboy fervor in him.

There was a short stretch of time when my mother wasn't all the way out of her marriage to Sal, yet my dad was very much on the scene. One afternoon, when she was boating with Sal and his friends, Lamar got wind of it. He flew overhead in the Cessna 206 and dropped handfuls of yellow roses—her favorite—down on the boat. My mom tilted her head back to watch the plane as it slowly circled. Yellow roses rained down. Sal knew who my father was, and that he'd been seeing his wife. He yelled insults up at the plane and threw the yellow roses overboard. My mother hid her smile behind her hand.

Sal wouldn't let her leave without a fight. If my father used charm to woo her, then Sal used money to keep her. After the roses, Sal bought her a brand-new Corvette, bright orange with a T-top. The car was beautiful, but it wasn't what she needed. She packed up her things and moved in with a friend, taking the Corvette with her. A few weeks later, the Corvette disappeared from the parking garage. She filed a police report and an insurance claim, but the car was never found. The chapter of her life with Sal had officially closed.

SOON AFTERWARD, LAMAR and Artis moved in together in an apartment on Miami's ritzy Brickell Avenue. My dad would have preferred a cabin in the Georgia mountains, but my mom's heart was in Florida. Miami, in particular. In the early 1970s many of Miami's neighborhoods still had a small-town feel. Coconut Grove, where my parents spent a lot of their time, was a hangout for artists, hippies, and beatniks. In the Grove, houses were painted in funky tropical colors. Chickens strolled the streets. The communities that would come to define modern Miami were just being established, and the Miami that is famous today—largely built on the drug trade and influenced by the TV phenomenon of *Miami Vice*—wouldn't arrive until a decade later.

Around this time, my parents exchanged a pair of matching necklaces. My mother's was simple—a black bear claw set in silver on a silver chain—while my father's was more ornate: a grizzly claw set in gold with a smooth oval of moss-green turquoise at the top. He wore it on a gold chain around his neck with the claw pointed toward his heart for good luck. From then on, he wore it every time he flew.

IN 1973, AS soon as their divorces from Sal and Nancy went through, my parents were married in the backyard of Art and Jewel's little house in Clewiston. Art's gardenias perfumed the air. With this marriage, there was no white wedding dress trimmed in lace. No bridesmaids dressed in pink. No groomsmen in tuxedos. This time around, my parents were wholly themselves. My mother wore a traditional Seminole wedding gown, a nod to the Seminole women in her family and the Miccosukee culture she had admired from her childhood. The dress was made by a close family friend, a seamstress who lived on the nearby reservation. Her dress was in two parts—the top part a yellow cape that slipped over the head and draped from the neck to the waist; the bottom, a long, flowing black skirt stitched with traditional *taweekaache* patterns in bright blue, green, yellow, and white. She went barefoot and wore her long hair loose down her back. My dad wore a bell-bottomed polyester suit with a ruffled shirt. His narrow face had filled in nicely, and the scars from his troubled skin had faded. They were a striking couple. Though they weren't flashy, they projected a hunger for bigger things that shone brightly even then.

In the photos I have from that day, my father's face wears an expression that recalls the earlier black-and-white photo taken with Nancy and their three sons. The crinkled eyes and the grin are the same, but now, instead of smiling at something far in the distance, he's looking right in front of him. I can't ignore the confidence in my dad's stance, his square-shouldered way of meeting the camera with his whole body. He doesn't look like a man who is worried, though by all accounts he should have been. He was newly divorced, with an ex-wife and three children to support, he had a young wife accustomed to a finer lifestyle than he could provide, and he'd just signed a lease on an expensive apartment on Brickell Avenue. Though he was a professional pilot making good money, it wasn't enough.

For my father, it would never be enough. The early poverty in Wrightsville, the beating with the switches in the front yard, the horrible scarring acne, the sense of being uneducated and less-than—all of that had settled deep in his bones. He would spend the rest of his life trying to feed what was eating him. He'd do it with women. He'd do it with money. He'd do it with power. He was propelled by a macho insatiability that was everywhere in the 1970s, from Burt Reynolds to muscle cars to the ongoing war in

Vietnam. It would carry the United States into the madness of the 1980s, paving the way for Wall Street scandals, the Gordon Gekko era, and the Ronald Reagan presidency. It would carry my father to the end of his life.

MY DAD HAD so little time left. Already the clock was ticking. Just twelve years from the day he married my mom to the day his plane fell out of the sky. Enough time to amass a fortune, to build an empire, to have another baby. Nearly enough time to see it all destroyed.

PART II

5

First Run

WHEN I ASKED PEOPLE ABOUT my dad, they'd sometimes wonder out loud what would have happened if he'd kept to the straight and narrow. They didn't have an answer, but I think I do. He would have chafed under the weight of an unexceptional life. A nice house, a nice boat, a nice vacation once a year? Ordinary comfort would never have been enough for him. No, he wanted to be able to buy Dom Pérignon by the case. He wanted to walk into a jewelry store in the Caymans and purchase a gold Rolex with cash. He wanted to own islands in the Bahamas. Maybe because that's what it took to counter his early years of deprivation and his ongoing feeling of unworthiness. Maybe the hole in his heart was so immense that he had honed an instinct to fill it with excess. Or maybe he was simply built different than other men.

At this point my dad was still a law-abiding citizen, just another straitlaced pilot for Eastern Airlines. But even if he wasn't involved in anything illegal yet, the world around him was laying the foundation for what was to come. The old saying went that a pilot always has too much time on his hands, so he either drinks or he gets into trouble. If that pilot was based out of Miami in the mid-1970s, the trouble he got into was smuggling. My dad's best friend, Ron Elliott, was smuggling lobsters in from Colombia. He'd pay the crew of a Colombian Air Force plane to offload the coolers in Miami, bypassing customs. Meanwhile, my dad's brother Tony was smuggling lobsters in from the Bahamas. He'd fly to the Out Islands and buy the lobsters from local fishermen, then flash-freeze them in an apartment in Nassau before flying them to restaurants in Atlanta.

By 1975, forget lobsters. Marijuana was the product to move. It was the 1970s, and everybody was smoking grass. A lot of the dope was coming in on boats, largely brought in by fishermen, shrimpers, and good old boys from coastal Florida. The fishermen and shrimpers knew the Florida coastline in detail, and the good old boys had grown up piloting the mangrove channels in johnboats before they were old enough to drive. They could outmaneuver anybody on the water. Flying in drugs was just starting, and the drug enforcement agencies hadn't caught up to the smugglers yet. The stakes were lower than they would be a decade later, but the money was still good. Really good.

It was the money that drew my dad. By 1975 he was strapped, owing Nancy all that child support and shelling out for an expensive apartment for Artis. He'd also gone in on a second plane with his brother Tony that the two rented out to skydiving crews on the weekends. The last pilot who'd taken the plane up came in hard and damaged the landing gear. So now my father owned a plane that needed fixing. It couldn't be rented out, and he found himself short on cash.

My dad kept his planes at the Opa-locka airport outside Miami. That's where he ran into a guy named Jack Devoe. Word around the hangar was that Devoe was running dope. One day my father approached him and asked if he could fly in a load. Like Devoe, Lamar had a reputation around the hangar. He was known as a top-notch pilot who wasn't afraid to take risks. Plus he was affable and easygoing. Devoe decided to give it a shot, offering to pay Lamar $8,000 for his first run. Eight grand was a fortune to my father, nearly a third of what he made in a year. The flight would be long and dangerous, but the payoff would be huge. Plus, he'd be getting paid to do the thing he loved most—flying.

That evening, he told Artis about his meeting with Jack Devoe.

"This is what I'm thinking about doing," he said. "I need the money."

My mother listened carefully. She is an excellent listener. That night, she didn't offer an opinion one way or the other, though she's a woman with strong opinions. She let my dad sort it out for himself, weighing the pros and cons out loud. Internally she was worried, less about the legal implications and more about the flight itself. Nobody flew a single-engine Cessna over that much water, especially not at night. It was beyond risky, but she knew my father well enough to know that the risks wouldn't deter him. If anyone could do the impossible, it was him. When my father decided that he'd do the job for Devoe, she quietly supported him.

THE NIGHT OF my father's first gig, my mom baked him a Cornish hen. She wrapped it in tinfoil and then a dish towel and put it together with a bunch of bananas and a gallon jug of water. My father was filled with nervous anticipation as he dressed for the flight—long pants to keep his legs from sticking to the seat, a pair of deck shoes that he could easily slip off, his black leather bomber jacket because it gets cold at altitude. My mom kissed him goodbye, and he drove to the airport in Opa-locka.

Jamaica is nearly six hundred miles from Miami, almost due south, a four-hour flight in the Cessna 206. Even that is enough to make most people sweat, but there was a bigger problem: Cuba sits in the way. In order to fly over Cuba, Lamar would have to log his flight with Cuban authorities. But this particular trip needed to remain off any official government books. The stakes of encroaching on Cuban airspace were high, especially in the wake of the Cuban Missile Crisis. Russian-built MiGs were known to buzz private aircraft that got too close. My father would have to fly around Cuba, skirting the island to the east, adding about two hours to the journey each way.

He took off from Opa-locka near midnight, after the control tower at the small regional airport had shut down for the day. In some ways, flying at night was better. There was less air traffic, and it was easier to stay awake without the sun baking the plane. But night flying could be treacherous. The lights on boats looked like stars, and it was easy to get disoriented. Storms were harder to see at night, and without advance warning a pilot could have trouble navigating around them. But on this night, the night of my father's first gig, he had a clear run.

For the first leg, he kept Andros Island to his left and Cuba, far in the distance, on his right. Navigating by the stars and a series of aviation maps that he would periodically unfold across his lap, he followed the chain of the Bahamas southeast, past the Exumas, where dark water stretched beneath him, hiding the wrecks of crashed planes. The runways on those islands were too short for many pilots. A plane might get overloaded with cargo or the wind might come from the wrong direction or the pilot might misjudge the distance to takeoff, and the plane would climb into the air briefly before dropping to the sea below.

I imagine that my father was considering the risks of his own flight: fuel trouble, mechanical failure, thunderstorms, a too-heavy load. But I bet he held those risks up against the $8,000 waiting for him back at the hangar. He would have counted that money in his head a thousand times during the flight, and he would have had it portioned out before he hit Jamaica, each dollar carefully spent. Everything I've learned about my father tells me that he was strategic and methodical, especially when it came to money. He'd put some away for Nancy and the three kids and some would go to Artis for their day-to-day bills, and still there'd be a lot left over. He'd be considering strategies to invest it.

My father flew like that for hours, in a meditative state, alert to any trouble while his mind pondered. Pilots tell me that the only real times for worry are on landing and takeoff. The rest of the journey is mind-numbingly boring. Three and a half hours into his flight, he passed Grand Inagua, the southernmost island of the Bahamas. The landscape was silvered by moonlight as he headed due south through the Windward Passage. He scanned the sky for US naval aircraft from the base at Guantanamo. Like the Cuban MiGs, the US jets were also known to buzz unregistered private planes.

By now he'd been in the Cessna for close to five hours. Back in Miami, in the apartment on Brickell Avenue, my mother was still awake. She sat on the black leather couch in the living room, anxiously flipping through magazines and waiting for the telephone to ring with word of trouble.

My father cleared Haiti and passed over Navassa Island, just three miles wide and flat as a tabletop, inhabited by thousands of red-footed boobies. Then he turned due west for the final hundred-mile stretch to Jamaica. By now, the sun was rising. I bet he was still thinking about that eight grand and how he'd invest it. Capital assets, he'd decide: land, boats, more planes. As he neared Jamaica's eastern coast, the island's Blue Mountains rose in the distance, flanked by clouds. He stayed clear of Kingston, with its air traffic towers—this was still an undocumented flight—and headed north toward the agricultural land of the island's western territory. Past Ocho Rios, he pointed the plane inland, away from the water, and passed through Jamaica's Cockpit Country. Verdant and mountainous, Cockpit Country looked like an egg carton someone had turned upside down. It was filled with swooping hills and valleys, and there was nowhere to land, not a flat piece of earth anywhere. He listened to the sound of the engine with a close ear, alert to knocking or coughing or any other sign of trouble. He kept an eye on the fuel gauge as it dipped toward empty.

I want to be with my father in the plane in this moment. I want to know what it felt like to see the sun rise over the green hills. Was he exhilarated? Nervous? Maybe neither. My dad's philosophy was straightforward: *Convince yourself that you're already dead. If you survive, you're ahead of the game.*

On the far side of that hilly terrain, an airstrip was cut into a sugarcane field. A single man stood at the end of the runway, flagging the plane in. It was early morning, but already the hot sun beat down. Lamar landed the 206 and shut down the prop. He stripped off his leather jacket. By now, men were appearing from between the cane stalks. Lamar stepped from the plane. His safety relied wholly on the competence and goodwill of the Jamaican ground crew—strangers to him, but he had no choice but to trust them. What he had in his favor was that he genuinely liked people, and they liked him in return.

With the eye of a pilot, Lamar watched the 206 being loaded, giving directions where necessary, the same as he did to his own ground crew for Eastern. The men were strong and fast. They knew how to move the bales quickly. His plane wasn't the only Cessna to touch down in those remote cane fields. Yet there were enough stories about overloaded drug planes crashing on take-off to make him wary. He called for adjustments in the weight balance and made sure the bales were shifted forward to make takeoff easier. He checked that there was enough room in the passenger seat for him to pull back on the yoke when he lifted off.

When the marijuana was loaded, the Jamaican ground crew moved barrels of gas close to the plane to begin refueling. This, my father would have watched nervously. There was a lot that could go wrong. If the barrels had been sitting outside overnight, half empty, fat drops of condensation would have formed on the walls of the barrels and dripped down into the gas. If water made the engine cough on takeoff, he'd go down in the sugarcane. Lamar would also have worried about the type of fuel they were using. Aviation gas has an octane rating of at least 100. If someone had accidentally swapped in a barrel of automobile fuel with an octane rating in the 80s or 90s, then the engine would run rough, fouling the spark plugs. Eventually it would overheat. I imagine my father nervously scrubbing his face with his hands, or at least wishing he could, perhaps hiding his worry from the men. It was a long journey over water from Jamaica to Miami.

Once the plane was loaded and the fuel bladders in the wings had been topped off, Lamar took off quickly, not lingering on the airstrip. He would have breathed a sigh of relief when the Cessna made it to altitude without the engine sputtering. Not until then could he be sure the fuel was good. He retraced his steps over Navassa Island, toward Haiti, through the Windward Passage, past Grand Inagua and its watery wrecks. By this stage of the journey, his most dangerous threat was fatigue. He'd been in the plane all night, for more than eight hours. The adrenaline thrill of reaching Jamaica, of loading the plane and taking off from a rugged airstrip, had subsided. The steady hum of the engine would have lulled him.

The sun rose higher in the sky, and he made the last leg of the journey in full light. Lamar kept the Cessna low over the water as he approached the coast of Florida and slipped into the state under the radar. He landed on an old dirt road north of Lake Okeechobee, where Devoe's crew waited to offload the bales of marijuana. No crew of his own—not yet. On this first run, he was only the pilot. They had the plane unloaded in less than two minutes. My father never even shut down the prop. He took off again as soon as the marijuana was gone, and the Cessna rose into the sky. He wasn't in the clear just yet. He might have offloaded the bales, but his cargo hold was strewn with bits of leaf and bud. He'd need to clean every inch of the plane before he was safe.

He headed to Opa-locka, just another 206 cruising the skies over Florida. He landed at the airport, climbed out, and stood on legs that had gone wobbly from hours of sitting. He shook them out, and after a few minutes he was loose and limber, his body freed from the plane and pumping with what felt like electricity. He cleaned out the Cessna, vacuuming up any evidence of marijuana seeds or leaves. He was meticulous. No trace of marijuana was left in the plane when he finished. Jack Devoe met him at the hangar with a paper bag full of cash. Eight grand, like he'd promised.

My dad tucked the cash into his flight bag and drove home to the apartment on Brickell Avenue, where my mom waited. She'd spent all morning worrying, still afraid the telephone would ring with bad news. She'd cooked him a hot meal, so he'd have something to eat when he got home, and a wave of relief washed over her as he walked through the door. Relief and, in no small part, disbelief. She poured him a drink while he stripped down and took a shower. Keyed up, he talked nonstop, narrating everything that'd happened in the last twelve hours. He was already thinking about the next run and strategizing how to do it better. The worries about fuel and mechanical problems and bad weather that had been on his mind during the long hours of his flight slipped away.

He sipped the drink slowly and sat back on the black leather couch. He closed his eyes and spoke about a future beyond anything he had imagined before, a future where eight grand was nothing.

WHAT MY DAD was doing was illegal, he knew, but he justified it by pointing to the marijuana itself. Grass was harmless, he believed. He didn't smoke it much—booze was his drug of choice—but he knew it had been smoked for thousands of years, originally as a type of medicine. Plus, Jimmy Carter, who'd just wrapped up a term as governor of Georgia and was preparing a run for president, was even talking of making it legal. To my dad, what he was doing didn't seem that bad, and it offered the opportunity for a whole new kind of life, the kind he'd always dreamed about. So he kept going.

In 1976 my father flew a total of six loads of marijuana into the United States, each between six hundred and eight hundred pounds. At the time, marijuana had a street value of anywhere from $20 an ounce for the low-grade shit to $350 an ounce for top-grade ganja. On the high end, he would have been transporting close to $2 million of marijuana in a single run. He got another paper bag full of cash every time he made the trip to Jamaica.

It would have made sense for him to keep his side business of running dope a secret, but my father loved talking about it. He liked telling stories and swapping tales, and in Miami in the mid-1970s everybody had a story about smuggling dope. Sailors at the wharf, pilots in the pilots' lounge—people talked. My dad's reputation around town as a daring, get-it-done smuggler grew.

But there were still people he kept quiet around, like my mom's parents, Art and Jewel. Even in the middle of his growing success, my dad knew he was striding a path that some people—good people he respected—would disapprove of. They'd stand by him, he knew, but he hated to disappoint them. He also didn't speak openly about the smuggling in front of his children, though my brothers pieced together what was happening. They were older now, fourteen and sixteen. Only my sister Jennifer, still a kid, didn't understand any of it yet.

IN THESE YEARS, my mom wore her role as stepmother like she wore most things in those days—with a cool, don't-fuck-with-me edge. She'd never be an archetypal mother figure, not in their lives or in mine. She didn't spend her afternoons in the kitchen baking cookies. She refused to sing lullabies or make a fuss over boo-boos. Artis valued toughness; she encouraged independence. The first time she met my father's boys was on a weekend parachute jump in North Georgia. Lamar and his brother Tony had been hired to fly the skydivers all weekend. Everybody stayed in tents. There was booze around the campfire in the evening, ribald talk, a heavy dose of adrenaline and testosterone. Artis laughed with Bill and Terry about Tony's women troubles. She treated them like adults. They thought she was incredibly hip.

Bill was a lot like our father: a firstborn son with a high dose of ambition and a brilliant mind. Plus, he had an advantage our father didn't have at a young age—someone close with a college degree. Lamar had failed out of the University of Florida after his first semester, but my mom had graduated from the University of Miami. It was her route out of small-town Florida and her introduction to the wider world. Years later, when I was a kid, she was still talking about the kosher delis in Miami and how she'd learned to eat pastrami on rye there. The University of Miami was not just an education for her; it was a path to better things. When

Bill, at sixteen, declared that he wanted to be a marine biologist, it was Artis who helped him with his college application. Bill applied to only one school: the University of Miami. My mom was confident it would do great things for her oldest stepson. More than anything, she knew an education would keep Bill out of the growing family business.

She wasn't opposed to the smuggling. She had faith in my father, and she understood his ambitions. Her biggest concerns were about the very real risks that came with the flights themselves, the danger of taking a single-engine Cessna over that much water in the dark. Each time my dad flew a gig, my mom waited up all night, fearing the call that he'd run into trouble. Each time he flew another successful run, my mother's worry lessened and my father's boldness—some might call it his hubris—grew.

But there was one person around Miami who wasn't singing my father's praises: his ex-wife, Nancy. She was still angry about the divorce, and more than anything she was upset about the current financial situation. Her marriage to my father had been marked by struggle and deprivation, and when they'd reached the middle class, she'd finally been able to breathe. And then he'd left for a younger woman and a glamorous lifestyle, and she still had three children to raise. Word of her unhappiness reached Lamar, and my dad—who wanted to be liked by everyone—chafed under her displeasure.

One day my mom decided to invite Nancy to lunch. The two women met at a café in Coconut Grove. My mother dressed in an elegant pair of long pants, gold hoops in her ears, a pair of sandals on her feet, her long hair hanging down her back. Nancy, too, wore her best, though Nancy's style was more conservative. They made polite chitchat over lunch, each woman curious about the other without the intervening filter of my father. Neither was catty nor cruel, and the lunch was, on the whole, pleasant. Nancy's only complaint was about money. There just wasn't enough of it, she said. The child support and alimony from Lamar didn't stretch far enough to cover three children. Artis listened attentively. As always, she kept her opinions close. By the time the waiter had cleared their plates, she was already formulating a plan.

"You need to give Nancy a chunk of cash," she told my father when they saw each other that evening.

"I already write her a check every month," he said.

My mother waved that away. "She needs a lot of money, all at once."

When my mom offered an opinion on something, my dad listened.

That's why one morning he got up early and drove to the house in Cutler Ridge where Nancy still lived with the kids. She answered the door in her bathrobe.

"This is for you," he said, handing her a brown paper bag.

"What's this?" Nancy asked.

"Look inside," Lamar told her.

Nancy glanced inside the bag. It was stacked with bricks of cash.

"Is that enough?" my dad asked.

Nancy, struck dumb, nodded.

It *was* enough. She never told anyone how much was in the bag, but she stopped complaining about my dad and money after that. She found a good job as a secretary in a doctor's office. Soon she moved up to office manager. She started dating and met the man who would become her second husband. When people around Miami whispered to her about my father, she just shrugged and changed the subject.

6

The Transportation Guy

BY THIS POINT FLORIDA WAS rapidly becoming the hub of drug smuggling in the United States. In 1977, if somebody needed a top-notch dope smuggler, they'd head to Miami. That's where my father was establishing himself as a go-to smuggler in the industry. Soon he cultivated a connection with a trafficker whose business was based in Colombia. But this wasn't like the early runs for Jack Devoe, which weren't much different from my father's Eastern Airlines routes. With the Devoe runs, he'd pick up cargo in one location and fly it to another. Then he'd collect a paycheck. Or, in this case, a bag full of cash. But with the new Colombian line, my dad wouldn't simply be a link in the supply chain. He'd be in charge of the entire smuggling operation.

Even in this bigger, expanded role, my father still saw himself as a good guy. He was simply moving a product from one place to another, he justified, like any other pilot transporting cargo. He didn't grow it. He didn't sell it. He just moved it. Later, when the feds were interrogating my dad about his role in the drug trade, he'd tell them—truthfully—"I was just the transportation guy."

His Colombian supplier intended to bring a huge amount of marijuana into the United States, much more than a few hundred pounds every couple of months. My dad needed a strategy for how to manage it. At the time, a lot of pilots—especially ex–Vietnam

War pilots—were discovering that smuggling pot into the States could make them a fortune. So they'd get their hands on decommissioned military aircraft, which could carry several thousand pounds of marijuana at a time. But large transport planes get noticed. In the 1970s, a transport plane headed from Colombia to South Florida would look suspicious. In one twelve-month stretch in 1974 and 1975, six planes that were smuggling marijuana crashed in the Southeast. Four of them were former military: a B-25 bomber and a converted navy patrol plane, both from World War II; a DC-3; and a DC-4.

My father took a different approach. He'd use the planes he already knew well, the Cessna 206 ("the Hulk") and a Cessna 207 that he called Captain America. Cessnas were reliable, and even more importantly, they were unremarkable. The 1970s had experienced an unprecedented wave of enthusiasm for personal aircraft, and the skies above South Florida were filled with 206s and 207s. They served as pleasure cruisers, easy aircraft to fly and maintain. Feds rarely expected them to be drug planes, in part because of the very real drawback of cargo weight. A Cessna 206 can carry roughly eight hundred pounds, a 207 around sixteen hundred. By comparison, a DC-3 can hold six thousand.

To bring in the amount of weight his Colombian supplier was intending, using only Cessnas, my dad would need multiple planes. He'd need more pilots. He'd need airplane mechanics and refuelers. He'd need a loading crew who could put the bales on the plane in-country and a catch crew who could pick up the bales in Florida. In short, he'd need to assemble an entire team. But this wasn't *Ocean's Eleven*. My father didn't have access to an international group of operatives. What he had was the people around him: the rangy Boy Scouts he'd grown up with, his brother Tony—who'd always been a ladies' man—and the women who circled around Tony. My dad knew pilots from Eastern, sure, but a lot of those guys were already running their own operations. Instead my father recruited pilots from his group of friends. Some were former military, some worked for small carriers. He recruited practically everyone in his circle. They'd be sitting at lunch or having drinks, and my dad would toss it out casually, like he was asking them to join his bowling league. Of course, some of them said no. But eventually his operation came to include many of his friends and acquaintances.

These weren't tough guys. None of them had done time (yet). They weren't drug users, though they might smoke a joint here and there. They were mostly young people from South Florida and rural Georgia who needed cash and were up for anything. They didn't have college degrees or career aspirations, but they knew their way around a sailboat and an airplane. They were willing to work hard. They had a high tolerance for risk. These early years in the drug trade, before the government caught up, would be remembered as the good old days, when money flowed easily and the danger seemed insignificant. Later, they'll talk about the smuggling years as the best years in their lives.

If my father had survived, if he'd been able to keep his operation small and safe, stay working among those he loved and trusted, maybe now he and I could sit and have a drink together, and he'd tell me all about it. Sometimes I imagine how I might be healed inside if I were able to sit with my father and be part of his world. But this is a dangerous train of thought. I want to be angry for the path he chose. I want to resent him for creating a life that put both strangers and the people he loved in danger. But I can't make myself feel any of that. All I feel is an overwhelming sense of loss.

The truth is, my father would never have kept his operation small and safe. It wasn't in his nature. He began fine-tuning it with each run. He learned to set up two catch crews fifty miles apart, one in the Everglades and one west of Lake Okeechobee. He needed both crews for the gig, but he based them apart in case one ran into trouble. If worse came to worst, one crew could manage alone. Sometimes a crew would wait in the parking lot of a gas station, smoking packs of cigarettes and listening for the call over the ship-to-shore radio. Sometimes they'd pretend to be fishing in the Everglades. They'd be ready and waiting for the signal to head to the drop zone. There were eight potential drop zones that my father used—roads, dams, pastures, private airstrips, and construction sites. He didn't know ahead of time which one would work best for that particular run. Local cops sometimes patrolled the back roads where smugglers like my dad were known to drop dope. Once an airboat full of tourists was parked smack in the middle of the drop zone. Another time, a police roadblock stopped traffic on a back road, looking for an escaped prisoner. It was the cover plane's job to watch for these threats. While a plane loaded with marijuana was flying in from the Caribbean, the cover plane would fly across the drop zone and check for activity on the ground. The pilot in the cover plane would radio the two catch crews over marine radio, since the standard aviation channels were too risky. The catch crew would toss their butts out the window or drop their fishing poles and head to the drop zone. The plane carrying the marijuana would land, and the team on the ground would pull open the cargo doors and start tossing the bales from the plane. The pilot would keep the prop running and take off again as soon as the hold was empty. The whole process, from landing to dropping the bales to taking off again, took less than five minutes. The gig looked a lot like my father's initial run, only now he wasn't the one flying the dope. He was in the cover plane.

It's staggering for me to imagine the coordination and smooth exactitude it took to pull off this kind of operation, especially in an era before cell phones, when pilots could only communicate by radio over frequencies that were accessible to anyone. Over time the operation grew smoother, savvier, and more complex. The crews had started by off-loading the dope into old pickup trucks, but then my father had the idea to buy a fleet of four-by-four working trucks. He had the new trucks painted green and stenciled with a logo for Florida Hyacinth Control, a company my father invented. Water hyacinth is a leafy green aquatic plant with purple flowers that proliferates in the fresh waterways of South Florida. It forms a dense, impenetrable mat across the water that chokes out the fish beneath and crowds out native plant species. It's been a bane across the Florida landscape since the early 1900s, and the state is forever trying to eradicate it. On one particular gig when my father was flying cover, he watched from above as the catch crew loaded the bales in the back of one of the Florida Hyacinth Control trucks. The dope plane took off, and the truck headed toward the highway, but my father spotted a police cruiser in the drop zone. He radioed the guy driving the Hyacinth Control truck to give him a heads-up. The guy driving the truck—a nervous man they called Frog who was always worried about the drops—weighed his options. He could turn the truck around and head in the opposite direction from the police cruiser, but he thought that would look suspicious. He decided to stay the course and press forward. As he neared the police cruiser, the patrol car slowed and lowered its window. Frog also slowed, trying not to think about the eight hundred pounds of marijuana sitting under a tarp in the back of his truck.

"How's it going?" the police officer called out to him.

"Pretty good," Frog said.

"You seen anything back the way you come? Thought I saw a plane flying low."

Frog shook his head. "Haven't seen a thing."

7

Monopoly Money

AS MY FATHER BROUGHT ON more pilots, he was able to take more and more steps back, distancing himself from the dope they flew in. He went from flying the marijuana himself to flying cover to managing the gigs from a remote location. He missed the thrill of being in the pilot's seat, but he was growing more cautious as the feds got savvier at tracking down smugglers. He was always there, though, when it was time to hand out the money.

People still talk about my father's payoff parties at the Mutiny Club in Coconut Grove, the slick hedonistic hotspot that had become the headquarters of Miami's drug scene. The Mutiny's guest list read like a who's who of smugglers, dealers, celebrities, and politicians, with everyone from Richard Nixon to Don Johnson on the roster. The club's suites were decorated in lavish themes like a Balinese rain forest and a Japanese ryokan. Roman baths and mirrored ceilings popped up in more than one. The valet line out front was filled with Ferraris, Porsches, and Maseratis. At the height of its popularity, the Mutiny sold more bottles of Dom Pérignon than any other place in the world.

When it came time to pay his crew after each gig, my father rented two adjoining suites at the Mutiny. He had the kitchen send up a spread of steak, lobster, and sandwiches. There was as much booze as anyone could drink: Maker's Mark for Tony, Stoli for the ground crew, Bud Light for the mechanics, and Bacardi Añejo for my father. The whole team came to the party—pilots, catch crews, mechanics, and drivers. This was an easygoing crowd of marijuana smugglers, without the hair-trigger tempers or drawn guns famous in the cocaine trade.

My father would intentionally arrive late. He let his crew enjoy the food and drinks in the suites for a while. When he finally showed up, he carried a large duffel bag. The payoff parties were celebrations, but they also served as business meetings. The crews brought up any problems they had during the run and suggested techniques to improve the next haul. Then, while everyone watched, Lamar dumped the duffel bag onto a table. It was full of cash—roughly $500,000—with the money banded in $5,000 bricks. As his crew ate and drank, Lamar circled the room, speaking to each person individually. He carried a small sheet of paper.

"Listen," he might say to someone. "You did good on this run. I'm going to have you drive point on the next one. You're owed twenty thousand, but I'd like you to take twenty-five."

After these conversations, the person he'd been speaking to walked to the pile of cash and took the amount they were owed. My dad never touched the money. When the last person picked up their cash, there was nothing left in the pile. It always came out even. Lamar had a brain built for quickly adding and subtracting sums. No one needed to double-check his math. It's what made him a good pilot, a good navigator, a good carpenter, and a good leader of an operation like this. He didn't have a second-in-command. There was no lieutenant in his operation. He had people who worked for him, people he assigned jobs who were higher or lower on the scale, but there was only one boss, one voice, one man in charge.

Can you see it, the kind of authority he wielded, even then? Can you appreciate how naturally he stepped into his role, how easily power came to him, this kid from Wrightsville who once fished golf balls out of ponds filled with alligators to sell back to rich assholes? This is my dad, I want to say. Look at him. He's not nobody. He's a big fucking deal.

MY DAD'S CREW wasn't the only group paying out at the Mutiny. Before one of the payoff parties, after he checked into the hotel, Lamar had to leave for a couple of hours. He left his brother Tony to keep an eye on the duffel bag of cash. Tony had been alone for about an hour when the fire alarm sounded. He called down to the front desk, and the woman on the phone told him the entire hotel was being evacuated.

"Use the stairs," she said, "not the elevators."

Tony grabbed the bag of money and a handgun, and he started down the windowless concrete stairwell to the ground floor, ready to keep a low profile and protect his cash. But when he looked around, he wasn't alone. The stairwell was full of men just like him, each with a single bag and a handgun tucked into the waistband of his jeans. At the bottom of the fire escape, hotel security directed everyone to the pool area. The men stood around, eyeing each other, holding tight to their bags. After a minute, they all began to laugh.

"What a great time for someone to try and rob us," one of them said. "We couldn't even file a complaint."

CASH FLOWED SO frequently and in such large amounts that everybody got to be casual about it. They started playing all-night Monopoly games using real dollar bills. They bought cars and boats and airplanes. My dad ordered Dom Pérignon by the case and opened bottles at breakfast. He bought a gold Rolex with a blue face and a diamond bezel at a jewelry store in the Caymans. He picked up a brand-new Cadillac. He ordered a mink coat for my mom and a matching one for my grandma Jewel. He took them both to Hawaii. Then he sent Grandma Jewel to Paris on the Concorde. My dad was still flying for Eastern at this point, and though my grandparents must have realized that his lifestyle far exceeded a pilot's salary, they didn't ask any questions. What mattered, more than anything, was that their daughter was happy.

IT WASN'T LONG before the sheer bulk of cash coming in got to be a problem. A million dollars in hundred-dollar bills can fit in a small briefcase. Put the same amount in twenties, and it'll take two large coolers. Smaller bills than that, and you might as well rent a U-Haul. The drug business didn't lend itself to crisp, large-denomination bills fresh from the bank. The payments came in all denominations, and there was a lot of it. My dad needed a place to park all that money. This is how he started to work with Lance Eisenberg, a Miami tax attorney with a knack for hiding funds offshore. Their relationship would be hugely lucrative for both men, but in many ways, my father's association with Eisenberg would spell the beginning of the end for his operation—and his life.

Lamar found Eisenberg in the way that a lot of people found each other in the smuggling community of Miami in the 1970s—a friend of a friend who was in the business. Eisenberg was originally from Long Island and Ivy League–educated. He favored linen pants, Hawaiian shirts, and loafers. He drove a white Mercedes. He was married, but he wasn't shy about chasing women. After he met my father, Eisenberg took private flying lessons and got his pilot's license. He crashed twice in the time they knew each other, both times coming into the runway too high and too fast. Lamar and Eisenberg were friends—good friends, even—but there was a rivalry between them. Eisenberg envied my father's easy masculinity and his magnetic charm. My dad envied how Eisenberg moved through the business world, a man at home among college-educated elites. Nevertheless, or perhaps because of this, they made a good team.

Eisenberg became my father's moneyman, and together they managed the proceeds from the drug smuggling business. One of the first steps Eisenberg took was to set up a series of bank accounts for my father in the Cayman Islands. My father would send someone from his crew to deposit cash in the accounts. It didn't matter what day of the week or what time of day the money arrived—a single phone call, and someone from the bank would meet him. This wasn't simply a courtesy; it was smart business. The bank charged up to one percent to count and deposit the money.

Once my uncle Tony went to Grand Cayman with a bag of cash. He flew commercial, and it was just like at the Mutiny in Miami: all the smugglers recognized each other. Tony got off in Grand Cayman on the morning's flight with a bunch of guys just like him—young, dressed better than they ought to be, a hint of backroads Florida still on them. Each of the guys carried a single suitcase. When Tony passed through customs in Grand Cayman, the agent asked him what was in the bag.

"Money," Tony said.

The agent waved him through.

He flew back to Miami on the afternoon flight, surrounded by the same group of guys that had been on the flight that morning. This time, their bags were empty.

But Tony didn't make many commercial runs to Grand Cayman. Before long, my dad had to rent a Learjet to move the cash. There was just too much of it.

8

"That's Not Chicken Feed, but It Will Buy a Lot of It!"

IT TURNS OUT THERE'S A limit to how many mink coats and Cadillacs a man can buy and still feel satisfied. At least, there was a limit for my father. He was strategic and goal-oriented, and once he began making serious money, he realized it was the moment to take the next step in his dreams. He might have spent a large part of his life in Miami, but my dad was still a country boy at heart. He never shook the memories of Ma Dell's and those fog-covered mornings in Wrightsville. Georgia would forever be a special place for him.

That's why in 1977 he bought a five-hundred-acre estate in North Georgia at the foothills of the Blue Ridge Mountains. He called the property My Goal Farm. On it, he built an eleven-thousand-square-foot house with two tennis courts, a ten-car garage, a hangar, and a swimming pool. He kept his planes in the hangar and bricks of cash in the root cellar. The house was a single story, though the ceiling in the great room reached to twenty-two feet. Sunlight poured in through floor-to-ceiling windows and spilled across hardwood floors. A Swarovski crystal chandelier hung in the formal dining room above a custom-built table that sat twelve. In the master bathroom, he installed an enormous sunken Jacuzzi. It sat six. My father also built a guesthouse down the road for my grandparents, Art and Jewel, and farther up the mountain he built a house for Pop and Pop's fourth wife. My father owned everything from the sloping bottom of the mountain to its top. For the first time in his life, all the land that he could see belonged to him.

I wish I could ask my father what it felt like to hold the deed in his hand. Did it scratch the itch of poverty in the back of his brain? Did it finally make him feel whole, despite the danger of what he was doing? Would he have said that it was worth it?

NORTH GEORGIA WASN'T like Florida in the late 1970s, where it seemed like everybody was smuggling dope and my dad could tell his stories openly, with panache. But even so, Cleveland, Georgia—where my father built his farm—was no stranger to outlaws. The town of four thousand is perched at the edge of the Chattahoochee National Forest. Neighboring towns fill with tourists during the summer months, but the little farming community of Cleveland is small enough that most would-be visitors pass it by. The Scotch-Irish immigrants who settled there in the late eighteenth century were clannish and tight-knit. From the old country, the settlers had brought a special talent for brewing homemade liquor. They could turn just about anything into whiskey. They called their brew moonshine because it was made in secret, under the shining light of the moon. An old joke has a traveling salesman ask a local, "Can you tell me where I can get some of that good whiskey you all make up here?"

"Sure can," says the local. "See that little church over on the hill?"

The salesman shades his eyes to see the church better. "You don't mean they sell whiskey over at that church?"

"Nope," the Georgia man says. "That's the only place they *don't* sell it."

But there was trouble for moonshiners starting in the mid-1800s, when the Internal Revenue Service was created to collect taxes on luxuries like alcohol and tobacco. The moonshiners in the mountains of North Georgia refused to pay, and Revenuers, as the IRS agents were called, made it a personal mission to hunt down stills. Tension between shiners and the law ratcheted up through Prohibition, when stills dotted the hillsides throughout the Blue Ridge Mountains and into Appalachia. Chases between moonshiners and tax collectors were legendary. Stock car racing evolved out of these car chases, and eventually NASCAR was born. The mountains around Cleveland lay claim to several well-known moonshiners, like Pete Roberts. People say if Pete Roberts liked you, you got the good stuff. If he didn't like you, he let you have the lesser stuff. And if he didn't know you, he didn't give you any stuff at all. The stretch of highway in front of My Goal Farm had once been known as Pete's Strait.

Which is all to say that my dad's neighbors in Cleveland might have been curious about what the good-looking pilot was doing with the airstrip on his property, but they weren't particularly concerned. It was simply business as usual in the mountains of North Georgia.

BUT EVEN IF someone had gotten curious, my dad had a fantastic cover story. Since 1945, poultry has been Georgia's largest agricultural product, and a billion-dollar-a-year industry. Broiler chickens hold the number-one spot in the list of top Georgia commodities by value. And Cleveland sits just thirty minutes south of Gainesville, Georgia, known as the Poultry Capital of the World. Let's just say that if a man needed to launder a lot of money—I mean, a *lot* of money—then a capital-intensive enterprise with a highly perishable product that turns over every six weeks would make a great investment. So my father launched a chicken operation.

Not long after my dad bought My Goal Farm, the *White County News* featured a front-page story on his chicken business. The article showcases a five-inch-high photo of my father, looking dapper in a shearling-lined leather coat and blue jeans, standing in front of the Piper Cub. The photo sits under the headline "Experimental White County Farm Trying Wood Heat for Chickens." He'd just installed a new chicken coop on his property, a 450-foot behemoth outfitted with his own innovations. According to the article, those innovations drew poultry executives and scientists from all over the world. "Chester believes it may be the largest and most modern chicken house ever built," the article says. "Last week, when word of his new features spread throughout the huge International Poultry Show in Atlanta, he had visitors from as far away as Africa." My father encouraged anyone who was curious to come out to the farm to see his projects. "My gosh, of course we want people to come and see what we're doing," he told the *White County News*. "We're working hard, but gradually all of our dreams are coming true."

And he wasn't faking it. The chicken business might have been a front, but my dad genuinely enjoyed farming. That was one reason why his neighbors liked him. He was a hard worker who could spend all day on a tractor, just like the men who owned the neighboring farms. They saw him in the fields with his hay baler and speculated on how his newest batch of chickens was doing. Once a snowstorm blew in when a neighbor and his wife were gone for the day, and their cattle were left stranded in the field. My dad spotted a little calf in the snow and trudged across the field to drape it in his coat. When the farmer and his wife got home, they spotted the calf—and they recognized the coat. They took it back to Lamar with thanks and teased him that the calf would have been just fine.

My dad shrugged sheepishly. "I thought it was a newborn."

That story got traded all around Cleveland. The farmer's wife told her friends about it when they stopped by for a cup of coffee. "He's a man's man," she'd say. "But he has a soft heart."

My dad liked being outdoors. He liked building and fixing things. Mostly, he liked innovating. In the house, he installed a pulley system at the top of the stone wall in the front room that he used to hoist up a massive Christmas tree each year. He experimented with solar panels—a new technology then—and built radiant floors heated by the fires that burned in the stone fireplaces. These technologies were light-years ahead of anything at the time, partly because he had the money for it but mostly because he had the curiosity, the vision, and the know-how.

The article in the *White County News* went on to detail the other forward-thinking projects on the farm, like his herd of beefaloes, which were bred for a meat that was low in cholesterol and high in protein. It talks about the vineyards my father planted with the intention of building a winery, and his acres of Christmas tree crops. He was exploring alternative energy sources, and he'd installed a large telescope for his astronomy projects. The article even mentions the house itself, its high ceilings, three large fireplaces, tennis courts, swimming pool, ten-car garage, and the two prominent local architects who helped design it.

What's missing in all of these descriptions is any mention of drug smuggling, and it's hard to say just how much people in the community knew at this point. But I think they had their suspicions, because I see it at the edges of this article, like a wink and a nod between neighbors. "While the farm is taking shape, Chester is supporting his experiments with timber from his land, his knowledge of airplanes, and a series of developments elsewhere." Did the reporter know just what those developments elsewhere were? I can't say for sure, but the final paragraph feels a touch cheeky. "Rebuilding airplanes is a major fundraiser as well as a hobby for Chester. For instance, he has recently purchased, for $3,000, a US Customs chase plane that crashed in the line of duty. When he puts it back together again, he figures to sell the craft for $35,000. That's not chicken feed, but it will buy a lot of it!" A crashed US Customs chase plane bought and fixed up by a drug smuggler? People tell me my dad had a great sense of humor.

FOR THE MOST part my folks weren't like the people in Cleveland, Georgia, a town of salt-of-the-earth farmers who had been in the mountains of North Georgia for generations. I'm sure there was more than one conversation about them held over a plate of fried chicken at Ma Gooch's restaurant in town. There was certainly talk about my glamorous mother, with her designer clothes from Atlanta. There were even whispers about how she liked to sunbathe nude beside the swimming pool. People knew she had been a teacher, though she'd quit when they left Miami. She was kind to everyone but carried herself with an air of mystery and a cool distance. It was hard to get to know her.

My dad was much more sociable, and unfailingly courteous. He didn't run his flights too early in the morning or too late at night, so the engine noise wouldn't bother the hardworking people around the farm who were up early to tend their animals and crops. He would have liked to put lights on the runway, but he felt that would be disrespectful.

My parents made friends with a few of their neighbors, mostly transplants like them who also didn't fit the North Georgia mold—potters and craftsmen and artists. These couples would come over for long, boozy dinners and late-night games of cards. Sometimes they'd all end up in the swimming pool. Or the Jacuzzi. But most of my parents' friends came from their smuggling circle.

My dad and his best friend, Ron Elliott, who had his own successful smuggling operation by this point, used to play a game when they were flying. They'd make plans to meet up, but they wouldn't say where. One would give the other a series of clues from the landscape, like a scavenger hunt, and the other would have to puzzle out the meetup location. Ron had been hassling Lamar for months to see the farm, but my dad kept putting him off, telling him, "Wait until it's finished." Finally Ron said, "I'm coming up there." Lamar agreed, but instead of giving him an exact location, he gave him a series of clues: head toward the town in North Georgia that's the same name as a town in Florida, then drop low between the set of magnificent breasts. Ron pointed the nose of his plane toward Gainesville, Georgia, and as he neared the town, he dropped his plane low until he spotted a pair of hills in the distance. He flew toward the low peaks and looked out the side window of his twin-engine, but what he saw below looked like a resort—tennis courts, a swimming pool, a sprawling house. Just then he heard the signal that Lamar used over the radio. Two clicks and then Lamar's voice, greeting Ron how he always greeted him. "Hey, boy."

"Where the hell are you?" Ron asked.

"I'm looking at you. You're coming right toward me," Lamar said.

"No, that's a resort."

Lamar chuckled. "That's it."

"What about a runway?"

"There's a runway running down the field."

Ron brought the twin-engine in low and slow.

"You sure there's a runway down here?" he asked my father over the radio.

"There's a runway," my dad said.

Ron dropped the plane down in the grass, and true enough, there was a fine, smooth runway. He slowed the engines and taxied toward the house, where Lamar stood on the porch, pups stretched out around him.

"What do you think about that runway?" Lamar asked as Ron walked up.

Ron shook his head. "Hardly looks like there's anything from above."

My dad clapped him on the back. "That's a trick the CIA boys taught me."

Ron glanced at my dad, but he kept his mouth shut. Later this line would take on new weight.

9

Bill, Terry, and Jen

WITH THE MOVE TO NORTH Georgia, my dad saw his children less. His oldest, Bill, was at the University of Miami on a premed track. Bill's plans to be a marine biologist had gone out the window the first time he stepped into a research lab at the university's medical school. He'd seen how the marine biology department had to beg for funding. The medical school, on the other hand, had cash for research in spades. It was an easy choice.

My sister Jen was turning into a teenager—witty, beautiful, and stubborn. She spent summers and Christmases on the farm. Our dad would fetch her in his plane, but more often than not he'd end up flying her back early. They excelled at aggravating each other. Jen had been born in the midst of grief and divorce, when her mother's attentions were turned inward to sorrow over Richard's death, and our father's focus was on building a new life elsewhere. My sister often felt ignored. That feeling turned her bold and confrontational in a bid to be noticed. She'd challenge our father regularly. When he told her to call him "Sir," she retorted, "Were you knighted by the queen?" When he was angry at her, he'd growl, "You're just like your mother."

Terry, meanwhile, was trying to carve a path between his brilliant older brother and his brazen little sister. He charted a path that wavered between people-pleasing and trouble-making, trying each one on to see how it fit. He was into chess, and the chessboard came out every time Terry visited the farm. Our dad was the better player, but Terry was strong too. He was also gifted in an airplane, another Chester who was crazy about flying. When he turned sixteen, Terry soloed and got his pilot's license. That's when everything changed between him and our father.

Until that moment, the smuggling business had been an unspoken secret between Lamar and his sons. Our dad didn't talk about it with them openly, and my brothers didn't ask. But marijuana smuggling was everywhere in Miami, and their father had gone from living in a three-bedroom ranch house in suburban Cutler Ridge to a five-hundred-acre estate in the mountains of North Georgia. They knew he'd given their mother a paper bag full of cash. It didn't take much to piece it all together.

After Terry got his pilot's license, our dad suddenly opened up. He started talking about the business whenever the two of them flew together. Lamar wouldn't lead the conversation, but he'd respond openly if Terry steered him toward it. He told Terry everything—about the runs to Colombia, about the catch crews waiting in the Everglades, about the money making it to the Caymans. Throughout these discussions, Terry convinced himself, there was always an undercurrent of promise. Terry was sixteen, barely more than a kid. Our father possessed a magnetism that made people seek his approval, and his middle son was no exception. Terry longed for his attention, often had it, and was jealous of anyone else who got it. Our father had taken Terry into his confidence—not Bill, not Jen—and one day, Terry was sure, he would be invited into the business. Not just invited in, but welcomed as our father's right-hand man. Terry knew he was bright, capable, and a good pilot. He would be the natural choice. But once, in the cockpit, our father admitted to Terry what he thought about the smuggling business. "Smuggling is for losers," he said. "Dirtbag guys who can't make it any other way."

That didn't make sense to Terry. Our father wasn't a loser. He was living the kind of life people dreamed about. Terry couldn't see what our father already knew, and what we, his children, would spend a lifetime learning—that money would never move him up in class, especially if he made it by smuggling drugs. Our dad wanted for us what he never had for himself: the kind of middle-class respectability that comes from a college diploma. That's why, instead of asking Terry to join the operation, he sent him to college at the University of Tennessee.

But Terry wanted nothing to do with college. He wanted to be alongside our dad, running the business. At least one good thing came out of his time there: he met the woman he'd marry, a pretty junior named Leigh. Leigh had the kind of intelligence, insight, and self-possession that it would take to weather the years ahead.

"You're going to fall for my dad," Terry told her excitedly before their first visit to the farm. "Everybody does."

But Leigh turned out to be one of the few women who wasn't susceptible to our father's charms. She had enough remove to see how Lamar treated Terry, and the idea that drug smuggling might be something to aspire to was beyond her. Where other people saw Lamar as a dashing, charismatic renegade, Leigh saw him as manipulative and ultimately unconcerned with the welfare of his son. Lamar was using Terry, she believed. The coming months would confirm her suspicions.

One night over Christmas break, when Terry was at the farm for a visit, Lamar pulled out the chessboard. It was a black-and-white onyx set my mother had bought for him. He poured himself a drink and set up the board on the table. Terry took a seat on the opposite side of the board. Lamar was an excellent player.

But Terry had spent the better part of his first semester playing chess against excellent players. He beat our father quickly in two back-to-back games. Lamar went quiet, and Terry briefly considered throwing the third game. That would be a bigger insult than winning, he decided. He'd waited his whole life to beat his father at chess. He went ahead and won the third game. Lamar sat at the table for a single beat, staring at the chessboard. Then he swept the black and white pieces onto the floor. The pawns clattered to the ground. A bishop snapped in half. Lamar stood. Without speaking, he stalked to the bedroom and slammed the door. Terry sat in the living room by himself and stared at the board, too stunned to say anything.

My father wanted his children to be like him—exceptional—but he still needed to be the master in his own domain. His ego and the vein of competitiveness that ran through his life wouldn't allow for anything less, even when it came to his own son.

IT DIDN'T TAKE Terry long to quit the University of Tennessee. By the summer, he was finished with his stint in college and ready to step into the family business. But he still wasn't invited in. At least, not right away. He moved into the guest bedroom at the farm, which would forever be "Terry's room" after that. Instead of smuggling dope, Terry dug ditches. He worked hard labor for months. It was penance, he knew, for dropping out of college. But one day our father relented. He came down to the field where Terry was working and called his middle son over to him.

"I need you to fly the Hulk to Seattle," Lamar said.

The Hulk—which had survived the crash in the Everglades—needed to be outfitted with special equipment for short takeoffs and landings, called STOL equipment. The manufacturer was based in Seattle, and Lamar needed the plane moved out there. Terry was a pilot, though he hadn't been in a plane for over a year, and he'd never flown the 206, which was bigger, faster, and more powerful than the Cessna 150 he'd trained in. Yet Terry, raised by our father, never had *can't* in his vocabulary. He would sooner die trying to fly the Hulk than tell our dad he couldn't.

As far as Lamar was concerned, he wasn't sending his son on an impossible mission. He was offering him a shot at something bigger. Terry had been floundering since he flunked out of college. Lamar knew his boy's potential, and he believed in his abilities. A flight like this—long, challenging, extreme—might be just the thing Terry needed to propel him into the life he was capable of. For Terry, that meant a role in our dad's business. And though Lamar wanted more for his middle son, he was coming to accept that Terry would join his smuggling operation. In that way, the Seattle mission was a proving ground.

The evening before Terry took off for Seattle, Lamar gave him a quick rundown on the Hulk, pointing out the instruments that were different from those in the Cessna 150. He also gave Terry a set of high-altitude navigation charts, the kind airline pilots use, marked only with interstates and city names. They were nothing like the sectional charts used by private pilots for navigation.

The next day Terry took off from the runway on the farm. He spread out his first high-altitude chart, opened his compass, and took a heading. Before long he realized he was headed in the wrong direction. After fumbling with the map a bit longer, he simply pointed the nose of the plane westward and followed the setting sun.

He flew six hours that first day. When he stopped at small airports along the way to refuel and get something to eat, people were shocked by his age and inexperience. Terry just grinned and tossed back his mop of blond hair. He was flying. There was nothing finer. And it sure beat digging ditches.

By the third day, the terrain was changing significantly. He'd been trained to fly in South Florida, where the highest elevation is a midden mound. As he landed in Cheyenne, Wyoming, there was a forty-knot crosswind and the specter of the Rockies in front of him. He watched a tumbleweed roll across the runway as he refueled. He took off again, flying higher and higher to avoid the mountains below. Glen Campbell's "Wichita Lineman" came over the AM radio, and he sang along, thinking of Leigh back in Tennessee. Like our father, Terry wore a bear claw around his neck when he flew. Terry'd had his own made. It was set with silver and red coral. He'd touch it as he flew, reminding himself of his mission. When his fingernails started to turn blue from oxygen deprivation, he knew he needed to drop the plane lower.

On the other side of the Rockies, he pointed the nose toward Seattle. Thick clouds covered the landscape. Like most pilots, he preferred sight flying. Flying by instruments alone made him nervous. As he approached the city, he came down through the mountains, where carcasses of crashed planes lay scattered along the slopes.

He thought, *I can handle this. This is my chance to show Dad what I can do.*

He thought, *This is nuts. This is insane. This is crazy.*

He thought, *This is wonderful.*

Terry's fuel gauge was almost to zero. He considered for a moment that he might be in trouble. Then the clouds parted enough for him to see the road below, and he reasoned he could always land on the highway, if it came to that. But then up ahead the lights of Seattle came into view, and Terry pointed the plane to the airport.

The man who greeted him—a burly bald guy in his thirties who worked as a salesman for the company installing the STOL equipment—was shocked to see Terry. The man was used to wining and dining his clients. He didn't know what to do with this kid, who wasn't even old enough to drink. He put Terry up for the night and then drove him to the Seattle airport the next morning. The manufacturer needed two weeks to install the STOL equipment on the Hulk, and Terry flew to Atlanta on a commercial flight.

The whole flight back, he anticipated what our father would say. Terry had done it. He'd accomplished Lamar's mission. He was eighteen years old, and he'd flown across the country in a Cessna 206. Terry—often overshadowed by his ambitious older brother or lost to the needs of his younger disabled brother—had done the impossible.

Our father picked him up at the airport in Atlanta. They talked about the flight, about Seattle, about the STOL equipment. But the praise Terry had been waiting for never came, not on the ride back to the farm or afterward. Instead, Lamar put him back to work digging ditches.

Our father could be a hard man. He had an undeniable gentleness, which he'd brought to bear with his son Richard and that he'd later bring to me. But he was tough on his two oldest sons. It rolled off Bill, who was independent, sure of his path, determined, and less explicitly interested in pleasing our father, but Terry admired our dad and desperately wanted to be seen by him. Yet parents often have a knack for withholding exactly the thing we need. Instead of turning toward Terry, Lamar turned away.

Two weeks later, Terry was back in Seattle to pick up the Hulk. This time he knew the route. He'd already experienced flying through the Rockies. He could take his bearings as he flew across country. Terry had many things running through his mind, but his main thought was for showing our father his worth.

Terry left Seattle with the Hulk in the late afternoon. He crossed the Rockies headed east, and he made it to Denver before dark, where he stopped and refueled. He wasn't tired, so he pressed on. He landed in Oklahoma City just before midnight. He got fuel and decided to keep going. He flew into the moon all night. He never stopped to rest. He remembered the conversations with our dad when Lamar had spoken openly of the smuggling business. Our father had bragged about his all-night trips to Colombia, the long hours in the cockpit without sleeping. Terry wanted to show Lamar what he was capable of. He wanted him to see that he could press on and make the entire trans-America flight in a single night with no copilot. *Look at me, Dad. I'm just like you.*

Terry landed the Hulk at the farm in Georgia twenty-seven hours after he left Seattle. Our father was surprised to see him. Terry wasn't supposed to be back for days. Exhausted, Terry stumbled to bed. He needed rest. Days of rest. He was sure that, this time, our father would acknowledge the great thing he had done, the marvelous feat of flying he'd accomplished.

Lamar woke Terry after only two hours of sleep.

"I need you to fly the Hulk to Miami," he said.

Terry had done the incredible twice already—he'd flown to Seattle in a plane he didn't know, and he'd flown back in a straight-shot flight, pushing himself to the edge of exhaustion. Now Lamar asked for a third impossible task.

IT'S EASY TO imagine this final flight demanded by our father as an initiation, the last torturous step before Terry could be welcomed into the business. Some might even see it as a kind of hazing. I'm able to have grace for my father here—because our relationship was different and shortened; because I'm not the one he treated in this way—and so I can acknowledge that he was raised in an era when being hard on a son was the accepted way to make him thrive, when turning away instead of turning toward was considered good parenting, especially for boys.

Terry had qualities that felt unique among our siblings. He possessed an edge, certainly, but he was also compassionate and kind. Perhaps our father saw that and worried. He was intent on making his children in his own image, and Terry had too much of something else in him—softness, maybe—for our father to feel easy about him. He tested his son, over and over, pushing him to the same extremes that he pushed himself.

In the end, Terry proved his mettle. He flew the Hulk to Miami, falling asleep and jerking awake the whole way, and afterward he was finally invited into the smuggling business. He began flying gigs as part of the team.

BILL, ON THE other hand, had set out on a path that our father approved of, a path that was about as far from our dad's poor beginnings as someone could get. In the summer of 1978, Bill graduated from the University of Miami and was accepted to the university's medical school. In the summer between graduation and starting med school, Bill got married to a young woman who was also attending medical school in the fall. After the wedding, the pair flew to the farm to stay for a week. My parents picked them up at the airport in Atlanta. On the drive back to Cleveland, Lamar was excited and nervous. He smiled the whole ride. When the truck turned in to the long driveway that led to the farm, he announced, "We got you a wedding present." A shiny new red-and-white GMC Jimmy sat in front of the house.

"Do you like it?" Lamar asked.

Bill stared back at him, shocked. The Jimmy was extravagant.

Our father wouldn't stop beaming. Here was his oldest son, about to start medical school, and he'd just given him a brand-new truck, paid for with cash. They say upward mobility in America is a myth, but in this moment my father must have felt as if he was on his way to making it.

And he was only getting started.

10

The Islands

BY 1978, MY FATHER WAS quickly becoming a major player in the international drug scene. A lot of people were smuggling dope in those days, but few did it with the kind of precision he brought to his operation. The newspapers were full of stories of one-off smugglers. A couple of guys would get their hands on a large transport plane, hoping to make it rich in a single run. They'd fly in five thousand pounds of marijuana but crash-land on the side of a mountain in Georgia or Tennessee before they could offload the bales, and the police would be on them in no time. It happened again and again. Not many of them had my dad's tactical mind. In fact, he was dedicating so much time to his smuggling business that he couldn't fly for Eastern. He requested a year-long leave of absence from the airline, citing hearing loss. He said his years as a jet mechanic had taken their toll. It was a minor problem, he told his boss, but it was interfering with his work. The truth was, he was busy with a massive new undertaking.

Fuel had always been a challenge for the smuggling runs, and now that my father and his crew were flying more frequently, it had become a major problem. Safe refueling locations between Colombia and Florida were hard to come by, and the pilots were worried about getting busted if they landed. Plus, they didn't trust the fuel in the out-of-the-way locations where they stopped.

They'd been lucky so far, but if my father was going to continue to grow his business, he'd have to establish a base where his planes could refuel from a trusted supply.

At this point, there were rumors that a drug smuggler named Carlos Lehder had purchased Norman's Cay in the Exumas, a remote chain of Bahamian islands roughly two hundred miles southeast of Miami. Lehder worked for Colombia's Medellín cartel, and he was responsible for shipping huge quantities of cocaine from South America into the United States. Norman's Cay was the perfect refueling point. It was halfway between Colombia and Florida, and the Bahamian government had a long history of looking the other way when it came to foreign criminal activity on its shores. When my father heard about Lehder and his Bahamian operation, he reached out to Lance Eisenberg, his moneyman, and floated the idea of buying property in the Exumas.

"I might know someone who can make that happen," Eisenberg said.

Eisenberg introduced my father to a man named Don Aberle, a Bahamian citizen born in Australia, who was president and controlling shareholder of a Bahamian bank called Columbus Trust. Aberle had founded Columbus Trust in 1963, and it had become a lucrative money-laundering operation. Aberle arranged for my father to buy five islands in the Bahamas—Big Darby, Little Darby, Goat Cay, Guana Cay, and Betty Cay. The purchase was made through a shell corporation called Caribe Shores, which kept my father's name off the deed.

Big Darby was the largest of the five islands, at 554 acres. In the 1930s, the island belonged to a British hotelier named Guy Baxter. Baxter received Big Darby as a gift from King George VI, who ushered Britain through World War II. Baxter built an enormous castle on Big Darby. It had turrets and colonnaded walkways. He installed stained-glass windows and shipped in mahogany furniture from South America. He grew palms for their oil and cotton, tropical fruit, and vegetables. In addition to his crops, Baxter also raised cattle and livestock. He would have been an unremarkable gentleman farmer, except that he was also a Nazi sympathizer.

A deep channel ran between Big and Little Darby. It was short enough to swim, but wide enough for a sailboat. Wide enough for a motorboat. And—as it turns out—wide enough for a German U-boat. During World War II, when Nazi submarines cruised the Atlantic, Baxter supplied their U-boats from his dock. The German boats would approach in the dark of night, and Baxter would transfer fresh produce and meat to their holds. For this, he was paid well by the Nazis. Eventually, after the war ended, he moved to Nassau—his grave is in a cemetery there—and Big Darby was sold. The island passed through several owners before my father purchased it.

Less than a mile from Big Darby sat Goat Cay, twenty-three acres total. My father never did anything with the small island, though in 2003, almost twenty years after my father's plane crash, husband-and-wife country music superstars Tim McGraw and Faith Hill bought Goat Cay. They brought in sand to make beaches, and they planted coconut trees along the shore. They built a house that was featured in *Architectural Digest*, and they flew down regularly, landing beside the island in their seaplane. Sometimes I wondered if they told stories about the drug smuggler who used to own it, the way we told stories about Baxter. But when my dad bought it, Goat Cay was just a strip of limestone rock, as exposed and open as a moor.

My father's third island was Guana Cay, seven acres total, not big enough for much, a stretch of sharp-edged limestone and sand. Then there was Betty Cay, with its single acre, only a footnote in the Darby Island sagas.

Which left Little Darby, the jewel in my father's crown, his pride, the island he transformed from a 238-acre stretch of wilderness into the staging ground for an empire. Little Darby ran three-quarters of a mile long from tip to tip. The topography of the island might be described as a set of wings, the kind children draw to depict a bird. At the midpoint, on the leeward side, facing the channel where Nazis once ran their supply boats, my father built a dock. On each of the two wings, the two high points extending to each side, he built houses. To the south, a guesthouse. And to the north, at the highest point on the island, a vantage point that overlooked both the dock and Big Darby, he built the main house, a house of imagination and careful engineering. It was set into the side of a hill, with a hangar for his planes underneath, just like at the house in Georgia.

The house itself had an open floor plan for its four thousand square feet and twenty-foot-high ceilings. There was a kitchen, a dining area, a sunken living room, and a bar. Nautical maps hung on the walls, and shells from the beaches lined the counters. The entire main house was outfitted with sliding glass doors. Anywhere he looked, he could see the water that surrounded the island. From the sunken living room, a trio of sliding glass doors led onto a concrete deck. From that deck, he could watch the Atlantic Ocean on the windward side, where the water was white-capped. Three bungalows radiated outward from the main house—a master bedroom and bath and two guest bedrooms and baths. The bungalows stood on pilings twenty feet above the ground. Each bungalow was connected to the main house by raised walkways. The effect was like something the

Swiss Family Robinson might have built, if the Swiss Family Robinson were drug runners.

On Little Darby, a runway led away from the main house. The runway was key. It was extremely short. There were not many planes—or pilots—who could land there. At the end of the runway, a path off to the right went down to the dock. Another path went straight ahead toward the southernmost tip of the island. Along the way, it crossed a series of beaches, each a postcard-perfect scene.

After my father bought Little Darby, he set about developing it with all the tenacity and determination he brought to his other projects. He had bulldozers and front loaders sent in on barges. He shipped supplies from Nassau. Building our new home on Little Darby, my father did much of the work himself, sweating beneath the hot Bahamian sun. His days were long and filled with the racket of construction—the rumble of bulldozers, the thud of hammers, the high-pitched whine of saws. But in the evenings that racket stilled. The sun sank low in the sky, and the machines ground to a halt. The laborers dropped their tools and walked down to the dock, where they climbed into boats that took them home to neighboring islands. Lamar followed them to his sailboat, the *Darby Island Lady*, which was tied up at the dock. He climbed on board, and my mom poured him his first drink, a Bacardi and Coke, no ice. He drank it standing while he talked to her about the day.

When he finished his drink, he grabbed the bottle of Joy dish detergent from the back of the sink. On the boat, they had to conserve fresh water. He skipped a shower and headed to the shallow flats near the dock. It was still hot and so humid that breathing felt like drawing cotton into his lungs. The mosquitoes were a black cloud around his face. The salt water was warm but still cooler than the air. He waded into the clear water and let the day's dirt wash away. Joy was the only soap that foamed in salt water, and he'd learned the trick of a Joy bath from his Boy Scout days. He soaped up in the shallow water and waded to the place where the flats dropped off, right beside the dock. Sharks cruised the deeper water. A night wind would be coming up soon. He swam until the last traces of soap had washed from his body and he could feel the fatigue in his muscles. Then he stayed a little longer, his strong limbs and big frame moving through the water.

AS HE HAD in Cleveland, Georgia, my father quickly became popular with his neighbors in the Exumas. He spread his money around for local causes. He bought a new roof for the church at Farmers Cay. He funded a town dump. He paid for a bridge connecting Exuma to Barreterre. I have to assume the local Bahamians pieced together my father's true occupation. The islands of the Bahamas were long acquainted with brigands of all sorts. They'd been a haven for pirates during the late 1600s and early 1700s, and more recently they had implemented some of the strictest banking secrecy laws in the world—bringing pirates of a different kind to their shores.

Soon the Darby Islands needed a caretaker. My father hired Captain Jack Wright. Captain Jack was famous in the Exumas for sailing small, triangular-sailed fishing smacks, and he placed in the regatta every year. Jack was strong and muscular, his hands rough from working on boats. He spoke with a low, gravelly voice. He made the best conch fritters in the Out Islands. Jack brought his whole family with him to Darby. His wife, Millie, was short and heavyset, and could deliver the kind of look that pinned a person in place. But she was quick to laugh with my father, who could always draw her out. The couple had three children when they first came to Darby. Their fourth, Terrel, would be born six months before me, as wild and fearless as I was. They'd have a fifth, Perez—built thick like his dad with a deep voice even as a baby—while they worked on the island, and a sixth, years later, after my father died. They'd name their last baby T.L., after my dad.

THE DARBY ISLANDS changed everything. Now that my father had a midway point where he could refuel his planes, store bales of marijuana, and wait out bad weather, his operation grew exponentially. For comparison: on his very first run in 1975, my father flew in a load weighing three hundred pounds. By 1977, he and his crew were bringing in one thousand pounds at a time. But in May 1978—after he bought the Darby Islands—he moved eight thousand pounds of marijuana through the Exumas and into Florida in a single gig. In September 1978 he brought in ten thousand pounds. In January 1979, not even a full year after owning the islands, he moved twenty-one thousand pounds of marijuana into the United States.

The Darbys turned my father's midsize smuggling business into a major international operation. Soon they'd put him at the center of a scandal involving the Bahamian prime minister, bribes, and banking secrecy laws. Much later, they'd be the sole piece of property the US government couldn't strip from him. But he'd already be dead by then.

11

Operation Lone Star

WHILE MY FATHER WAS TURNING the Darby Islands into the center of a multimillion-dollar transnational drug smuggling empire, federal agencies were already laying the groundwork for his downfall. Ironically, their investigation didn't start with the drug business. It began in Texas, as a probe into oil price manipulation. A joint operation between US Customs and the Internal Revenue Service, it was named Operation Lone Star after the favorite beer of the assistant US attorney in Houston—and it would become one of the longest and costliest investigations in US history. By its end more than fifty businessmen, government officials, drug smugglers, and money launderers would be indicted; at least one witness would be murdered; a plot to assassinate a federal prosecutor would be exposed; and an assistant US attorney would be in jail.

Though Operation Lone Star was launched in 1979, its origins dated back to October 1973, when members of the Organization of Arab Petroleum Exporting Countries—OPEC—imposed an oil embargo on the United States. The embargo was in retaliation for America's support of Israel during the most recent Arab-Israeli conflict. Overnight, the price of oil in the United States doubled. Then it quadrupled. Lines formed in front of gas pumps as cars snaked down the street. The Dow Jones Industrial Average plummeted. The economy tanked. OPEC's embargo lasted for six months, until US officials were able to convince Israel to pull out of the Sinai peninsula.

One of the measures to come out of the oil embargo was an increased effort to develop domestic energy sources. That included drilling new wells. A classification system emerged in which domestic oil was categorized as either "new" oil or "old" oil. New oil was pumped from wells drilled after 1973 and was of higher quality. Its inferior counterpart, old oil, came from pre-1973 wells. New oil wholesaled for roughly $10 a barrel, while old oil sold for $5 a barrel. Which meant the playing field was ripe for illegal arbitrage. All it took was some logistical finagling to buy old oil at reduced prices and sell it as new oil using a falsified domestic crude oil sales certificate. In just one year, the Energy Department estimated that oil price manipulation tallied between $500 million and $2 billion.

In an effort to crack down on these cases, federal agencies launched investigations into domestic oil companies. One investigation in particular—Operation Lone Star—hit pay dirt. In March 1979, as the result of the investigation, the government issued indictments for the heads of two companies accused of conspiring to sell more than 750,000 barrels of old oil at new oil prices. Five top oil executives were arrested. They each faced a maximum sentence of twenty years in prison.

Twenty years for wealthy, well-connected Texas oilmen?

Please. That's not how this story goes.

The eighty-four-count indictment, which included charges of federal racketeering, was quickly dropped by a US district court judge. The judge insisted the indictment was too vague. It didn't do enough to explain the details of the crime, he claimed. The federal racketeering statute, the judge said, was "intended to keep racketeers out of business, not to make racketeers out of businessmen." And so the Texas oilmen were set free.

While the oil executives walked away from their charges, the federal agents of Operation Lone Star found something they were even more interested in—the money trail behind the oil deals. They discovered the man responsible for laundering illegal profits from the oil schemes and funneling cash through secret bank accounts in the Caribbean: Lance Eisenberg. It turned out that Eisenberg was laundering money for a lot of people, not just the Texas oilmen and my dad. According to Eisenberg's 1981 indictment, his clients also included the Colombo organized crime family in New York and a separate crime family in New Jersey.

Investigators eventually discovered millions of dollars funneled through the Columbus Trust Company in Nassau, the bank founded by Don Aberle, who had arranged the sale of the Darby Islands to my father. Columbus Trust was an umbrella firm for 450 shell companies, including my father's Caribe Shores. The bank handled money from a variety of illegal activities—oil price manipulation, fraudulent coal shelters, drug smuggling, and a number of businesses run by the mob. The shell companies were used to wire money back to the United States, laundered and ready to be spent. Investigators believed that Columbus Trust was initially funded by the fugitive American financier Robert Vesco, who had stolen more than $200 million from US investors (and was hiding out in the Bahamas). The Bahamian prime minister and a Bahamian Cabinet member were minor shareholders in the company, though they both denied any role in the way the bank conducted its business.

Operation Lone Star uncovered dirt on a lot of people, but my father—who by that point had become one of the most well-known and successful marijuana smugglers operating at the time—was a priority on the government's target list. The reason? The War on

Drugs. The War on Drugs had been formally launched in 1971 under the Nixon administration. It was a reaction to the 1960s counterculture movement and the widespread use of marijuana, especially by people protesting the war in Vietnam. Marijuana was seen by the establishment as a threat to American values. Nixon called it "public enemy number one." Marijuana was demonized, and those who brought it into the country were considered the worst kind of villain. By this time, my father's operation had grown to massive proportions. Between May and June 1979, his crew smuggled thirty-one thousand pounds of marijuana into the United States.

As a result of the Operation Lone Star investigation, the government held a series of grand juries in Houston. Agents began to subpoena witnesses. In response, my father assembled his own legal team. The first lawyer he hired was Jeffrey Bogart, a young attorney from Long Island. Bogart was in his early thirties when he worked for my father, but he'd already served as the assistant district attorney in Brooklyn, where he'd prosecuted organized crime and corruption cases. He'd moved to Atlanta and done a stint as the assistant district attorney there before going into private practice. Bogart had followed the money to the other side of the legal aisle, but he never lost his sense of right and wrong. His roots were working class, and he'd punched a clock in a factory before his legal career took off. But those days were long gone by the time he was hired by my father. Now bearded and bespectacled, he was more polished, less brash, with only an occasional *fuck* thrown in for good measure.

Bogart brought along another attorney, Mark Kadish, who came with a northeastern pedigree and a heavy dose of notoriety. Kadish had launched his legal career as part of the US Army's JAG Corps. In 1969 he was appointed defense counsel for the commander of the company of US soldiers charged with murder in the My Lai massacre in Vietnam. At My Lai, several hundred unarmed Vietnamese men, women, and children were killed by US soldiers. It was widely considered to be one of the most heinous moments of the Vietnam War, and it came to symbolize the brutality of the US role in the conflict. The commander Kadish represented was ultimately acquitted.

It's hard for me to stomach that this was one of the men defending my father. My dad's moral code was defined in terms that I will never fully understand. He saw himself as a good guy, yet he wasn't above associating with "bad guys" if they could help him in some way. Kadish had a proven track record with difficult cases. That's all that mattered to my father.

Even with Bogart and Kadish on his team, my dad was still worried. That's why he called in Bobby Lee Cook to serve as his lead counsel. Cook was a spitfire attorney from Summerville, Georgia, who held court like a preacher in the pulpit. He was famous for being unbeatable. His style was classic southern gentleman—tweed suit, wooden cane, pipe stuck in the corner of his mouth, chauffeured everywhere in a Rolls-Royce. He had the kind of folksy demeanor that juries loved and used expressions like *What's good for the goose is good for the gander* in court. Though Cook was ten years older than my father, he'd also grown up poor in rural Georgia. Both men had a fierce need to win. "He's the most vicious man I've ever known," my father once said about Cook. "I love him."

IF JIMMY CARTER had made it to another term, he might have legalized marijuana. But the newly elected Reagan administration was coming down hard on users, dealers, and smugglers. The administration fought drug use with policy and police activity, but its most effective tool was propaganda. Pot smokers became the scourge of American society. They were demonized as losers and criminals. Those associated with marijuana were just as bad, cast in the same shameful light. That included smugglers like my father.

Though the public hated anyone involved in the drug trade, in private circles, my father had made a considerable name for himself. The Ocean Reef Club in Key Largo was—and is—one of the most exclusive private clubs in South Florida. With a golf course, a marina, restaurants, and a private airstrip, it's the kind of place where the well-heeled congregate. My father had a membership and regularly landed his plane on the club's runway. It offered a good stopover point between the farm in Georgia and the islands in the Bahamas, and it was a swell place to have lunch.

Once, Lamar and his young attorney, Jeffrey Bogart, stopped at the Ocean Reef Club on their way down to Darby. The two men stepped out of the Cessna and slipped on sport coats. They walked to the Ocean Reef Club's dining room for lunch, dressed like any of the other diners in jackets and slacks, just a drug smuggler and his attorney. On the way to the table, a man with dark hair and heavy eyebrows nodded at my father. My father nodded back.

"Do you know who that was?" he asked Bogart as they sat down.

"I have no idea," Bogart said.

"That's Bebe Rebozo."

Rebozo was a businessman based in South Florida, and he was one of Nixon's closest friends and confidants. Here's my father, a poor kid from central Georgia with no college degree and no real refinement other than what money could buy, sitting in the Ocean Reef Club in a tailored jacket, acknowledged by a presidential adviser. He had, in that moment, reached an elite and seemingly untouchable circle.

But it wouldn't last. They'd let him in their club, and they'd just as quickly kick him out again.

12

Welcome to the World, Baby Girl

EVEN WITH THE FORCES OF Operation Lone Star aligning against my father, there was some good news on the horizon. At least, I like to believe it was good news. My mom had started waking up in the mornings sick as a dog. Her breasts grew heavy, and they hurt all the time. One morning my dad looked at her in the bathroom mirror and said, "Artis, I think you're pregnant."

My mom shook her head. "That can't be."

She had been told her whole life that she couldn't have children. Her mother was given diethylstilbestrol, or DSE, a synthetic estrogen prescribed to prevent miscarriages that was later found to cause infertility in the children of the women who took it. But it turns out my mom could get pregnant, after all.

She swears she was thrilled with the news. She says my father was, too. *You would have thought nobody but him had ever made a baby.* But other people tell me she was shocked and a little dismayed. She was only thirty-five at the time. On the older end of things to be having a baby, sure, but still young in the grand scheme of life. My dad had just bought her a brand-new Jaguar. Half the guys in his operation were in love with her. The maître d' at the Mutiny Club greeted her by name. She was having too much fun to slow down.

So was my dad. In the spring of 1980, in the weeks leading up to my birth, he flew to Colombia twice to arrange a major shipment of marijuana through the Darby Islands. I like to think he spared a moment to consider my mom, back home in Georgia, who would have been very pregnant with me—her first and only baby. I want to believe that's why he scheduled the smuggling run for late June, out of deference to her and out of excitement for me. I like to imagine that he wanted to wait to bring that load into South Florida until after I was born. Even though I was his fifth baby, I hope there was still something special in it.

I came into the world on June 11, 1980. The nurses swaddled me and passed me to my father, and he gazed down with all the tenderness of a new dad. "Welcome to the world, baby girl," he said. He pressed my mom to give me her name. He liked that *artis* meant "bear" in Celtic, and that the name connoted strength and loyalty to family. It wasn't long before he slipped my own bear-claw necklace around my neck. Mine was set with rough-cut turquoise the color of the sea. For my middle name he wanted Jewel, like my Grandma Jewel, and I became Artis Jewel Chester. But it was immediately clear that I needed a name all my own. My brother Terry suggested they call me A.J., and the name stuck.

Terry was nineteen when I was born. Bill was twenty. For my brothers, having a new baby sister was cool, if a bit redundant. They already had a little sister, Jen, born nine years earlier. Jen tells me she was glad when I joined the family. She says she always wanted a baby sister. I believe her. I love my sister. Our relationship is one of the greatest gifts I've been given. But I know that it was complicated for her when I was born. I arrived at the peak of our father's optimism, a new baby who would look on him with unclouded love. She tells me that he talked nonstop about how he was going to get it right with me. But it wasn't the same for her.

Once, when I was still a baby, my sister went to the bank in

Cleveland with our dad. The teller smiled at my sister and asked our father, "Who's this?"

"That's my daughter," our father said.

The teller looked genuinely surprised. "I didn't know you had two daughters."

There was my sister, ten years old and very smart, realizing that our dad had never once mentioned her.

BY THE TIME I was a few months old, Darby had become my second home. My mom would hold me in her lap as we flew down, or she'd tuck me into the back of the Cessna, surrounded by cases of beer and bags of rice (no car seat or safety device; this was the 1980s). Sometimes she'd hand me to my father, and he'd sit me on his knee while he flew, pointing out the islands below.

There is a Polaroid picture of my dad and me taken in the Bahamas when I was four months old. We're at the helm of his Boston Whaler. A trail of wake snakes behind the boat. Our hair is pressed flat against our heads by the wind, and the tip of Little Darby recedes in the background. My dad is shirtless, in a pair of cutoffs and aviators. I'm propped against the metal brightwork that frames the console. We both squint into the wind. My dad is smiling. He is forty-two years old, healthy and strong. He owns five islands in the Bahamas and an entire mountain in North Georgia. He has sailboats, airplanes, a bold and beautiful wife, four living children, and a circle of people who love and respect him.

I want to freeze my dad in this moment, to say to him, *Enough*. I want to tell him to cash out. Leave the business. Take his money and run. But how could I explain that to a man who was at the top of his world? It's October 1980. The grand jury hearings that will lead to my father's indictment won't begin until the following year. The first witness to be murdered won't die for another thirteen months. My father's death is still five years away. To him, the line between the good guys and the bad guys was still very clear.

PART III

13

The Drug Problem

BY THE EARLY 1980S, THE drug trade in the United States was ubiquitous. Everyone was involved, not just pilots and fishermen but policemen, judges, journalists, and politicians. The newspapers from that time are filled with stories of the arrests of sheriff's deputies, local TV news anchors, lawyers, accountants, and businessmen. Every strata of society had a hand in it. And everybody profited from it.

It hadn't taken long for Florida to become the epicenter of the American narcotics business. Though my father stuck to smuggling marijuana, cocaine was the product of choice for most smugglers. Cocaine was easier to transport than marijuana—less bulky, less pungent, more discreetly packaged—and the profits were astronomically higher. In 1980 a kilo of top-grade marijuana sold on the streets for $1,200. A kilo of cocaine went for $50,000. By 1981, seventy percent of the cocaine coming into the United States was moving through Miami, and the city became the staging ground for an increasingly violent turf war. The murder rate skyrocketed. In the national press it became known as Murder City. Miami had to lease refrigerated trucks from Burger King to handle the bodies that overflowed the morgue.

In response to the rise in violence, the state of Florida mandated stiffer sentences for drug smugglers. The law required minimum sentences of three to fifteen years and fines up to $200,000. "Florida desperately needs this penalty to deter smuggling and provide an avenue through which law enforcement can reach the higher ranks of smugglers," the state's attorney general said. The only provisions for reduced sentences were for those who informed on fellow smugglers.

Which made it a particularly bad time for my uncle Tony to get busted with a suitcase full of quaaludes and $40,000 cash. His version of the story is that a dealer friend of his couldn't make full payment on a shipment of marijuana, so he offered the cash and the quaaludes in exchange. Tony figured he could offload the pills, no problem. The dealer dropped off the suitcase and beat it out of there, and less than a half hour later the cops were busting down Tony's door. Tony swears he was set up. He probably was. The prosecutor offered him ten years of hard time, or he could roll on everyone he knew for a reduced sentence. Tony chose to roll. The good old days were officially over.

As part of his plea deal, Tony testified in front of the grand jury in Houston that was investigating Lance Eisenberg. So did a man named Al Rivenbark. Rivenbark was a loose associate of my father's, though I hesitate to call them friends. He was a stocky, squint-eyed front man for the mob who traveled with a bodyguard rumored to pluck out eyeballs. Newspapers called the forty-one-year-old Rivenbark "unsavory." There's a story about him that says that once, in Colombia, a donkey wandered onto the runway when one of Rivenbark's planes loaded with cocaine was about to take off. The plane swerved to miss the donkey and crashed on the runway. Rivenbark grabbed a machete and hacked the donkey to death.

There's another story about him—this one from my uncle Tony—that says Rivenbark once gave my father a husky as a gift.

The husky's name was Nikita. Rivenbark had met up with my parents at the airport in Opa-locka to give them the dog. What my father didn't know, according to Tony, was that Nikita was trained to attack on takeoff. So when the plane left the runway, the dog went berserk. My mom had such a gentle way with animals, Tony said, that she calmed the husky down. They flew the rest of the way to Georgia without incident, and Nikita joined the pack on the farm. She became my mom's loyal protector.

Tony's story about Nikita is up for debate (though he swore he was on the plane with them, and it's true that a husky named Nikita *did* live with us on the farm). What is not debatable is that Al Rivenbark worked for a New York organized crime family. He fronted a South Florida drug ring that imported marijuana and cocaine financed with mob money. Agents believed Rivenbark and Eisenberg had worked together to launder money skimmed from casinos by the Mafia. In October 1981, he testified for a full day in front of the Houston grand jury.

Rivenbark was subpoenaed to testify a second time, but on November 18, 1981, he was killed in a plane crash in Colorado. He was on his way to Black Mountain Guest Ranch, a luxury hideout that federal investigators said was known for hosting East Coast mafiosos. Two pilots were in the plane, plus Rivenbark and his bodyguard, plus another man and a woman. The plane left Miami that morning, refueled in Shreveport, Louisiana, and then, just after six p.m., three miles from their destination in Colorado, radioed air traffic control for runway conditions and a weather report. The runway was bare and dry. Broken clouds were scattered across the sky. The plane began its descent, but at 10,500 feet it neared a snowy cliff. The left wingtip sliced through a large pine tree perched on the edge of the cliff. The plane plummeted down the side of a ravine. The sheet metal of the airframe splintered into shards. Rivenbark and everyone else on board was killed.

The crash was ruled an accident, the result of pilot error. The National Transportation Safety Board report said it was most likely due to "improper IFR operation," which means the pilots misread their flight instruments.

This is the moment when my father's story begins to shift. It was easy to see his marijuana operation as a risky, adrenaline-fueled enterprise that turned out to be hugely lucrative for everyone involved. But the Rivenbark plane crash changed everything. This is when it sank in, for me, that my father was working with some very dangerous people. Rivenbark's plane crash might have been an accident, but the timing was suspicious, coming just a few weeks after his first grand jury testimony. That two well-seasoned pilots could both have misread their instruments is hard to believe. And Rivenbark was not the only grand jury witness killed.

Soon after Rivenbark's crash, prosecutors subpoenaed Sibley Riggs, a yacht broker in Fort Lauderdale, whom the newspapers called Rivenbark's girlfriend. A tall, striking divorcée with frosted blond hair, Riggs was popular, outgoing, and an excellent yacht saleswoman. She received a subpoena to testify in front of the grand jury in Houston, but she never made it.

On a sunny Monday morning in December, a maintenance worker at the Fort Lauderdale International Airport took a moment to admire Riggs's dark-blue Mercedes in the airport parking lot. "It was a real looker," he told police. When he stooped to pick up a piece of trash, he saw blood dripping from the trunk of the Mercedes. He called the Broward County sheriff's deputies assigned to airport security, and two officers rushed to the car. They pried the trunk open with a crowbar and found Riggs lying face down. Her lower legs were bent over her body, already stiff. They sprang up when the trunk lid unlatched. That's how the officers knew she was dead.

"She was brutally, brutally killed," a Broward County sheriff's detective told reporters. Friends had last seen her around three in the afternoon the day before, headed to show a yacht to a new client. She was killed early the next morning inside her Fort Lauderdale condo, beaten and tortured and then drowned in her tub. The sheriff's office didn't formally draw any connection between Riggs's murder and the ongoing Operation Lone Star case. "At first, we had a lot of roads to follow, but they led nowhere," the sheriff's detective in charge of the murder investigation told reporters. "We were never able to identify the mystery individual she might have been going to meet. We never found a suspect. We never found a motive. All I can say is that the case is still open and that we look forward to the day we can make an arrest."

The case was never solved. It was as if they didn't even try. Riggs was just another murder in Miami, and as a woman, she was a disposable victim under the rampant misogyny that underscored this world.

14

The Lesley Bickerton Affair

WHILE THE OPERATION LONE STAR investigation played out, my father put a halt to his smuggling operations. He turned his attention instead to developing a piece of land near the Chattahoochee River east of the farm, which he called the River Hills project. He planned to turn River Hills into the kind of campground where college kids could drink beer and float down the river. Like the chicken farm on the estate in Cleveland, it was another way of laundering illegal drug money. He hired a woman named Lesley Bickerton to work as his bookkeeper for the River Hills project. Bickerton was thirty-two at the time. She was a tall woman, soft-spoken, who wore large round glasses. The word people used to describe her, both to me and in newspapers from that time, was *plain*. And yet—something about her caught my father's attention. In addition to being his bookkeeper, she was also his mistress, though later when reporters used that term—*mistress*—my father balked. "She's just a girl I see from time to time," he said.

After our dad's death, my sister Jen tried to ask my mom about the affair, but my mom shut her down quickly: "Your father was the best husband anyone could ask for." Much later, when I asked my mom about Bickerton, her voice took on a hard edge. "We had too much else going on for me to worry about your dad screwing around," she said.

But that screwing around ended up playing a major role in what came next. Bickerton would ultimately become one of the most important witnesses in the federal case that government agents were building against my father. In 1981 the US Attorney's Office impaneled multiple grand juries in Atlanta with the intention of indicting him. These grand juries were separate from the Houston grand juries that had indicted Lance Eisenberg. Many of the people my father knew in White County, Georgia—bankers, car salesmen, reporters—were subpoenaed to appear before the grand jury. Importantly, so was Lesley Bickerton.

Her affair with my father was already souring by that fall. The reason? They'd had a disagreement about a dog. The exact story is hard to nail down because everyone has their own version. Even the name of the dog changes—newspapers said her name was Dobie, though Bickerton and my brother Terry have both said that she was called Kawena. The straightforward facts are that Bickerton owned a Doberman, and this Doberman was put in my brother Terry's care. Bickerton later claimed that she wanted her dog back, but Terry wouldn't hand her over. Terry swore that Bickerton had abandoned the dog. Wherever the truth lies, the outcome was the same: the friction over the dog led to trouble between my father and Bickerton.

According to newspapers, Bickerton left White County in October, the same weekend that River Hills opened. Reports said she'd attempted suicide and spent a week in the hospital before leaving the state of Georgia for a new life in Texas. But she didn't escape her troubles long. One afternoon in early January 1982, two criminal investigators from the Internal Revenue Service showed up, waiting in the lobby of a Houston accounting firm to confront Bickerton when she got back from lunch. The agents showed her their badges and told her something she'd guessed as soon as she saw them: they were there to talk about Lamar Chester.

Bickerton led the agents to an office, where they shared what they already knew about her. It was substantial. They knew that she'd lived in a trailer in the mountains of North Georgia near My Goal Farm. They knew she'd worked as the bookkeeper for the River Hills project. They showed her copies of her American Express bills. They knew my father had paid them. They knew she'd been his mistress.

All Bickerton would say was "I think I need an attorney."

One of the agents handed her a card. "If you change your mind and want to cooperate, you can call us."

On their way out the door, the agents had one more piece of business. They handed her a grand jury subpoena. Ultimately, Bickerton's reason for testifying against my father came down to one simple thing: her dog. It was the Doberman, not the subpoena, that made her ready to talk, Bickerton told agents when she called the number listed on the card.

BY THIS POINT, the Operation Lone Star investigation was in its third year. The initial probe into gas price manipulation had branched out into many separate investigations that involved businessmen, smugglers, and members of the Mafia. The case against my father had stalled without new evidence, but Bickerton changed everything. She gave investigators the most detailed portrait of Lamar and his organization to date. She confirmed that he made his money by flying marijuana into the United States. She told them that he claimed he was worth between $8 and $10 million, most of it tied up in capital assets. She said that he owned the Darby Islands, though his name wasn't on any of the documents and he had gone out of his way for years to make sure there was no proof that he was the owner.

Though she gave federal agents a lot of information about my dad, the most damning evidence was a paper trail that linked the money he made from drug smuggling to banks in the Caribbean. Bickerton's handwritten notes showed a direct flow of cash from a shell company in the Bahamas to Lance Eisenberg to Lamar. The notes contained specific details and exact sums of money. The money was then tied to his business ventures in North Georgia, including the River Hills project.

The only problem was that Bickerton's handwritten notes were fabricated. At least that's what she told a judge at a pretrial hearing in the criminal case against my father.

Bickerton claimed at the hearing that while she was being questioned by the assistant US attorney John Johnson and a US customs agent, Jeff Friend, she suggested creating and adding fake notes to the financial statements she'd already handed over to investigators. The fabricated notes would connect Lamar's money to illicit dealings and hidden accounts. They would also tie him to Lance Eisenberg.

According to Bickerton's testimony, Johnson and Friend were wholly in favor of this plan to doctor the evidence. And they didn't just want to use the fake notes to incriminate Lamar; they wanted to trick him into committing a crime. Before Bickerton left for the grand jury in Atlanta, she and federal agents photocopied the financial statements she'd given them, and then marked the originals with invisible ink. (Yes, invisible ink, like in a spy novel.) They gave the originals marked with the ink to Lamar's attorneys, along with the fabricated notes. The goal was to get Lamar and his attorneys to see how potentially devastating Bickerton's evidence was and tempt them to destroy the incriminating evidence.

Then, once they destroyed it, prosecutors could slap them with an obstruction of justice charge. (Johnson told his supervisors he had no knowledge of this scheme.)

But there was a wrench in the works: my father immediately recognized the notes as fake. It's unclear how. Perhaps because he knew Bickerton didn't take notes like that, or he realized that the notes contained details he hadn't mentioned in their business discussions. Or—and this possibility has been suggested by prosecutors, reporters, and people who knew Bickerton personally—she was acting as a double agent, still secretly working for my father, trying to trap prosecutors in a scheme that would ultimately get the case thrown out. It certainly was suspicious that she'd left North Georgia for Houston, which happened to be the headquarters of the Operation Lone Star investigation. Either way, Lamar's young Atlanta attorney Jeffrey Bogart, who possessed a finely tuned moral compass, had no intention of destroying the incriminating evidence.

What happened next is perhaps one of the strangest twists in this story.

Bickerton told prosecutors that she'd overheard a plot to assassinate John Johnson, who headed the Operation Lone Star investigation. After this story emerged, Johnson stepped down from his role. Which is perhaps another point suggesting that Bickerton could have been working as a double agent. Johnson was a fierce opponent; his resignation was a coup for my father's defense. As an added bonus, this left the Houston US attorney's office scrambling to appoint someone new to head the investigation.

They filled the post with a thirty-year-old prosecutor named Frank Robin. Robin was tall, dark-haired, and baby-faced. He liked bespoke suits and other fine things. "A man with expensive tastes without the pocketbook to support them," the chief prosecutor for the US Justice Department's Public Integrity Section would later call him.

Robin was hired in July 1982. Four weeks later, Bogart got a call from a man who identified himself as Charlie India. The initials—C.I.—were classic code for a confidential informant. "What I have, in the proper hands, could shut this investigation down," Charlie India said. He claimed to have proof of "outrageous" misconduct by both prosecutors and government agents in the case against my father, though he never specifically said what that proof was. "I've got information about some conduct on the part of the government that, if I was a federal judge, there would be some government attorneys and agents in jail," he told Bogart.

"You're talking about governmental misconduct?" Bogart asked.

"Absolutely," the man said.

"By the informants or the agents?"

The man laughed softly. "From the lawyers down to the informants."

He told Bogart that the Lone Star investigation under Robin's predecessor John Johnson had been using paid informants, which, though legal, is ethically questionable.

"They're on the government payroll," he said, "and they're all extremely close to Chester. I think their identities will surprise him."

One of the paid informants he was referring to was Lesley Bickerton.

In exchange for this evidence of misconduct—he never said exactly what it was, but he swore it would destroy the case against Lamar—Charlie India wanted $200,000. But Bogart wasn't buying. He had an internal sense of fairness guiding him as he navigated the complex legal and moral ground he was treading. He was, in Bobby Lee Cook's words, "a gentleman of impeccable reputation."

Instead of paying the $200,000, Bogart recorded the calls and turned them over to Justice Department officials. Agents for the Justice Department listened to the tapes. One of the most damning parts of the recordings was that "Charlie India" was familiar with federal prosecutorial jargon. For example, he called the Justice Department headquarters in Washington "main Justice," which is an insider term. The tapes were sent to Michael Fayad, a Justice Department official who was assisting the Lone Star investigation from Washington. A meeting was hastily called at Fayad's office to discuss the tapes. Frank Robin was at the meeting. As Fayad played the recordings for the Justice Department officials assembled in the room, he turned to Robin. "That sounds like a Texas accent. In fact, Frank, it sounds like your accent."

It didn't take Justice Department officials long to arrest Robin. It was the first time a Justice Department official had been accused of wrongdoing while working for the federal government since the US attorney general was indicted during the Watergate scandal.

Frank Robin's trial was held at the federal courthouse in Atlanta. The trial lasted eight days. The days went long, sometimes well into the evening, but my father didn't miss a single one. He sat in the fourth row, dressed in an expensive suit and gold wire-rimmed reading glasses, a yellow legal pad propped in his lap. He leaned forward when agents from the Justice Department testified. He took notes. The newspapers called him "quiet and unassuming," but it was when he was quiet that he was most determined.

Frank Robin was convicted at the end of the trial. He was disbarred and sentenced to ten years in federal prison.

THE TWISTS IN my father's case didn't end there. In another strange turn of events, Lesley Bickerton contacted Jeffrey Bogart that fall. Bickerton told Bogart that she also had information about prosecutorial misconduct. Though Frank Robin as Charlie India hadn't revealed the specifics of the misconduct, Bickerton did. She told Bogart about the handwritten notes she'd fabricated and the invisible ink. Bogart asked if she would agree to a videotaped deposition in which she'd admit to suggesting to federal agents that she falsify evidence. Bickerton agreed.

"What was their response to this idea?" Bogart asked in the deposition.

"Oh, they thought it was a great idea," Bickerton said. "I mean, it was like they just jumped at it immediately. They wanted to nail Lamar any way they could."

15

Darby

BY 1983 DRUG SMUGGLING THROUGH the Bahamas was a known fact. The island of Bimini had become a hotbed of smugglers and corrupt officials, and Norman's Cay—Carlos Lehder's island—was the headquarters for smuggling for the Medellín cartel. But the Darby Islands were still relatively quiet outside my father's circle. Among the sailing community, any whispers about Darby were about Baxter and his Nazi connections, not marijuana. Unlike the locals, those who passed through the Exumas didn't quite know what to make of the islands' owner, who by all accounts was a charming and gregarious guy with a chicken farm in North Georgia.

That May, Kevin Sealy and his family anchored off Little Darby for the night. Kevin was just ten at the time. His brother, Richard, was a few years older. Their parents had pulled the boys out of school in Canada and were spending a year cruising the Caribbean on their thirty-six-foot sailboat, *Nite Train*. Kevin and Richard had heard the stories about Nazis from other sailors, and the boys were looking for a swashbuckling adventure. The morning after the Sealys anchored off Little Darby, the boys didn't think anything of taking their Zodiac and pulling up on the island. Throughout the Exumas, sailboaters would often anchor on deserted beaches and go for a stroll or a swim. The chances of an island being unoccupied were high. On Little Darby, the boys poked around in the shallow flats and stood on the dock to watch the lemon sharks cruise below. They didn't know that my father had a direct view down on the dock from the main house. Sound carries across the water, and a conversation at the dock—or a laugh or even a sneeze—could be heard at the main house. When Lamar spotted the strangers on his island, he ran to the truck under the house and sped down to the dock. The truck bumped over the limestone rocks and came to a screeching stop at the water. The two boys froze.

"Who the hell are you?" Lamar said. "What are you doing on my island?"

He cut an imposing figure as he came toward them. The boys fumbled for words.

Kevin pointed to the sailboat anchored in the harbor and said, "That's our boat."

Lamar looked at the Zodiac they'd beached beside the dock. "Is that yours?"

Kevin nodded.

"Take me to your sailboat," Lamar said.

The two boys scrambled into the Zodiac, and my father followed. Kevin leaned over to his brother. "We're in so much trouble," he said.

When they reached the *Nite Train*, the boys' father, John, came up from below. Their mother, Sharon, was sunning on the deck. John gave the Zodiac a friendly wave.

"How's it going?" he called out to the tall man sitting in the bow.

Lamar's eyes roamed across the sailboat. He took in the Canadian flag and the couple in their early forties. He seemed to relax. Even with everything going on in his life, Lamar's nature was still open and friendly, like he couldn't help but be charming.

"You got any rum on this ship?" he called up to the Sealys. John laughed. "We've got some Bacardi below."

"Any Coca-Cola?" Lamar asked.

"Sure do," John said.

That was all it took. My dad joined them on the boat, and they spent the afternoon drinking rum and Cokes and swapping stories about the Exumas. At one point, my father mentioned that he was a multimillionaire.

"I've put over a million dollars into Little Darby alone," he said. "Now I'm investing in Belize. And I've got some important government connections in Nigeria."

"What about the US?" John asked.

Lamar shook his head. "I've got legal troubles there. Tax issues." But the Bahamas had been very accommodating, he said. "Hell, I just had the prime minister as my houseguest this weekend." He took a sip of his drink. "You want a tour?"

They set off to Big Darby first, where Lamar took them through Baxter's castle. They walked its rooms and snapped photos. On the way back to the boat, the two boys whooped at the big banana spiders strung on sticky webs between gumbo-limbo trees. Lizards slithered through the underbrush and rattled the dry leaves. Lamar pointed out the radio tower where Baxter had contacted German U-boats, and he explained the geology behind the island's limestone sinkholes. He stopped and knelt at a wild cotton bush and pulled off a boll for everyone to see. He cut stalks of sugarcane with a machete and sliced it in cubes for the boys to chew. He was his best self that afternoon—confident, full of knowledge, happy to share.

After the tour of Big Darby, he took the family up to the main house on Little Darby, where he showed them around. The boys gaped at the big-screen TV in the living room. It was 1983, and a big-screen TV was rare in most suburbs. To see it on an island in the middle of the Bahamas—

"This guy is something special," Kevin whispered to his brother.

In the kitchen, Lamar poured drinks, and the boys saw something that impressed them even more than the big-screen TV: an ice maker. They'd been on their sailboat for months under the hot Bahamian sun. Ice was an unimaginable luxury. The boys looked at each other.

"This isn't a normal island," Richard said.

Over cocktails, Lamar offered to fly them to nearby Lee Stocking Island in the morning for a sightseeing trip, and Kevin and Richard thought they must have walked onto the set of a movie. My father was true to his word, and the next morning he met the Sealys at the dock. He drove them to the main house and the Cessna 207 parked in the hangar. They all climbed into the plane, and my father took off from the runway. A rum and Coke sat on the dash as he flew. He circled Little Darby and then cruised over the top of the sailboat, close enough that the boys could see the screws in the hatches. Kevin pressed his face to the window.

"You want to take the controls?" my dad asked over his shoulder.

"Me?" Kevin said.

"Come on up here."

Kevin made his way into the front seat. Lamar gave him the controls, and the little boy flew the Cessna over the Bahamian waters. Forty years later, Kevin Sealy will still think of this day as one of the happiest of his life. He'll remember Lamar Chester as the coolest man he'd ever met.

In all his time with the Sealys, my father never once mentioned drug smuggling. But two months later, when the Canadian family turned their sailboat around and headed north, they were surprised when the gracious gentleman they'd met suddenly turned cold.

"This is the *Nite Train*," John Sealy radioed Little Darby. "We're passing by, and we'd love to stop in and say hello."

My father immediately radioed back over the ship-to-shore radio. His voice was stern. "Don't come to the island," he said. "Keep going."

The Sealys had heard enough rumors about drug smuggling in the Bahamas not to press my father. They heeded his warning and sailed past the Darby Islands without stopping.

I WASN'T ON Darby when the Sealys met my father, but I was there often. By the time I came to know Big Darby as a child, Baxter's legacy was on its last legs. His castle, once painted a pale sea-glass green, had faded in the sun. The concrete walls were crumbling, and exposed rebar poked through the ceilings. Horsehair mattresses were strewn here and there, their stuffing spilling from the inside. The furniture was long since gone. Vandals and thieves had stripped the castle of its wiring and fixtures, and goats had finished the work that the vandals had started. The goats disappeared eventually, mostly starved out, though every now and then someone would spot a rogue goat deep in the bush.

I rarely went to Big Darby. By that point it was too rough, too overgrown, but Little Darby was all I needed. I was wildly independent. "A hard little woman," Jack's wife, Millie, called me. By then, Millie's daughter Terrel and I were best friends. We were close in age, and we had the same tough, stubborn temperament. We were fearless about everything except sharks, which terrified both of us. We'd spend our days poking around the hangar or catching hermit crabs in the sand patch beneath the laundry line. If Terrel's older brothers were there, we'd head down to the dock and jump in the water while somebody kept an eye out for sharks. For lunch we'd come back to the house, and Jack would feed us pigeon peas and rice. When we got fussy in the late afternoons, Millie would send us away to one of the bedrooms, where we'd sit on the porch and look down toward the dock, the salty afternoon breeze warm against our faces.

I remember a day when my mom took Terrel and me down to the beach. We followed the runway to a path that led into the island's interior and then to A.J.'s Beach, which had been named for me, something that felt no-big-deal at the time. (As an adult, people will meet me and say, "Oh, you're A.J. of A.J.'s Beach," and that, admittedly, feels pretty weird.) The walk down to the water was shaded by coconut trees and tall pines. Terrel and I took off our shoes and ran, barefoot, down the limestone rock to the beach. The path was covered with pine needles, which were smooth underfoot, but also marble-sized pine burrs that dug into the balls of our feet. The sand was white with pink undertones. It felt delicious underfoot after the pine burrs and the rough limestone. It held our footprints long after we dove in the water.

And that water—it's the water of dreams. A clear aquamarine, the kind of water that gave rise to a thousand myths of mermaids and undersea realms. The beach was encircled by low cliffs, and these encircling arms kept the sea steady and smooth. We could see straight down to the bottom of the water, where silverfish flashed against the white sand. The water was the same temperature as our blood, and our bodies recognized it, like womb water. My mom sat on the beach and watched us play. After a while, Terrel and I came back on shore and the three of us set out for the far end of the beach, where a coral reef was tucked against the side of the cliffs. My mom handed us masks, and Terrel and I waded into the water. The big barracudas that hung out at the edge of the reef didn't scare us. We put our faces in. The coral was electric with tropical fish—blue tangs, angelfish, parrotfish. Purple sea fans waved in the current. We stayed close to shore, but it was enough to dip into that other world.

After A.J.'s Beach, we went to Coconut Beach, named for the hundreds of coconut trees that grew in the sand, more there than anywhere else on the island. The sand was coarse and dark on Coconut Beach. There was no place for swimming. The rocks extended too far from shore, and the waves were always rough. But the best shells washed up there, like conchs and tulip shells. They lodged in the crevices of the rocks, waiting to be found. We walked with our feet sinking into the hot, dark sand. Terrel and I picked up pieces of foggy sea glass that had been dashed against the craggy shoreline. We held them in our open palms for my mom to see. Sometimes whole bottles survived the journey to Coconut Beach with rolled notes inside, missives thrown into the sea like whispers into the ether, filled with longing and a desire for home.

Despite the beautiful beaches, my favorite spot on Darby was in the kitchen with Captain Jack. When he made fish stew in the mornings, he always saved me a fish head. He'd scoop grits into a bowl and ladle the spicy broth over them. I remember, once, after breakfast, Jack sat resting on the floor of the breezeway that circled the main house. He dozed with his eyes closed while a hot wind blew across the tops of the trees. Like my father, Jack was physically strong. He was an expert sailor, builder, and chef, but he had a soft side, especially with children. And though I loved my father first and most, I also loved Jack. I found him napping on the breezeway and crawled into his lap with a handful of plastic barrettes. Carefully, I stuck them in his hair so that we both had a head full of pink, yellow, and purple. He smiled sweetly at me, and I grinned up at him.

When I say I lost everything after my dad died, this is what I mean.

16

The Indictment

ON THE STRENGTH OF LESLEY Bickerton's evidence, in the fall of 1983 an Atlanta grand jury leveled a thirty-six-count indictment against my father. The indictment named eleven codefendants and forty-four unindicted coconspirators. Among the codefendants were Lance Eisenberg, my brother Terry, and my dad's best friend, Ron Elliott. The forty-four unindicted coconspirators had testified in front of the grand jury or provided other evidence in exchange for immunity or a lesser prison sentence, including my uncle Tony, whom they'd brought in shackled and dressed in his prison uniform. That's how the government was able to piece together information about my father's operation, including specific dates for drug runs and the amount of marijuana he'd brought into the country on each run. The indictment charged him with conspiracy, racketeering, money laundering, tax evasion, and drug trafficking. Along with the criminal charges, the government demanded forfeiture of all assets acquired as a result of criminal activity. Those assets included My Goal Farm, an orange grove in Florida, two boats, four airplanes, stocks, bonds, and cash, plus the Darby Islands. In essence, everything my dad owned.

The indictment was unsealed and presented on a Monday. My father turned himself in to US marshals that Wednesday. He was forced to surrender his passport and his pilot's license, and his bond was set at $1 million. He was allowed to sign for half of it without putting up any actual cash as security. The next $300,000 was covered by a surety agreement guaranteed by Nigel Bowe, his attorney in Nassau. The final $200,000 was a property bond on two homes in Florida owned by my grandparents, Art and Jewel—the modest house they lived in, and the little beach house on the Gulf Coast they'd scrimped and saved to buy in the 1950s.

This last part is hard for me to take. My grandparents had worked hard all their lives. It hurts to think of them putting their own property on the line to bond out my father, the drug smuggler. They had been staying at the farm in Georgia for the summer, like they did every summer. They lived in the guesthouse at the long end of the driveway, just past the cattle grate. No one asked them to put up their own house as part of the bond. They simply volunteered. "We're family," my grandpa Art said, and that was that. He drove with my dad to the courthouse in Atlanta, where he signed the paperwork, putting up the two houses, his life's investment. It was a measure of his character that not one of the federal agents or prosecutors who pursued my father so mercilessly was unkind to my grandfather in this process.

One of the lingering questions I have about my dad is why he didn't just flee the country. After all, he was the one who said to always have a landing spot in mind. And he had his own spot already picked out. He'd applied for Bahamian citizenship, and at the time the Bahamas had no extradition treaty with the United States. He could have simply put cash in a bag, climbed into one of his planes, taken off from our runway, and disappeared into the Caribbean. But if my dad had disappeared, he would have forfeited his bond. Among the other losses, his freedom would have come at the cost of my grandparents' life savings. They would have lost the house they lived in and the little beach house that was their retirement home. He weighed his own desires against theirs, and out of respect for Art and Jewel, he stayed.

AN INDICTMENT DOES not automatically mean a trial. There were still deals to be made. The other people named on the indictment were already hiring attorneys and speaking to federal agents, asking what it would take to get a reduced sentence. As for the house and the cars and the planes, the government would have to prove its case before it could seize those assets. Motions would have to be filed. Attorneys for the opposing side would contest those motions. The court system would grind slowly forward. While that was happening, my family would go on living in our house in North Georgia.

Meanwhile, my father's case was being covered in both the local and national media. The *Atlanta Constitution* ran an article titled "Drug Smugglers, Double Agents and a Woman of Mystery" with this lede: "After five years, a million-dollar federal drug investigation of a reputed smuggling operation that began in Houston has come to roost in Atlanta, taking on the characteristics—and the characters—of a classic detective novel." (The woman of mystery was Lesley Bickerton.) The *Nashville Tennessean* covered the hearings in detail. The *Gainesville Times* in Gainesville, Georgia, ran a five-part series titled "Citizen Chester." Even the *New York Times* printed stories. "Group in Bahamas Charged in Big Narcotics Conspiracy," ran one. "U.S. Tax and Drug Indictments Trail Figures in Bahamian Trust," read another.

My father didn't mind the press. In fact, he encouraged it. He held press conferences, wrote letters to the editor, and took interviews with reporters at the farm in Georgia. Again and again, my father promised journalists a story like nothing they'd covered before. He wouldn't give them the specifics—not yet—but he claimed it would shake the US government to its core.

17

The Bahamian Royal Commission of Inquiry

WHILE OPERATION LONE STAR INVESTIGATORS were tracing the money trail to pin down their targets, they kept running up against the same problem: the strict banking secrecy laws of the Bahamas. The United States had been pressuring the Bahamas for years to soften the regulations around its protected banking system. So far, the Bahamian government had refused. So the United States decided it would simply install someone who would. The goal became to oust much-loved and widely celebrated prime minister Lynden Pindling, known in the Bahamas as the Father of the Nation. Pindling had held office longer than any other leader in the Western hemisphere except Fidel Castro. Unlike Castro, Pindling had been democratically elected each time. He was first elected prime minister in 1967, when the Bahamas was still under British colonial rule. In 1973 he led the country to independence, transforming it from a colony to a free nation. In 1982, he was knighted.

As part of Pindling's tenure, he'd defended the Bahamian banking secrecy laws, which were some of the strongest in the world. This meant Bahamian financial institutions were under no obligation to surrender their records to anyone, including the US Internal Revenue Service. It was good business for drug smugglers like my father and for the mobsters who had turned the Bahamas into a gambling and tourist destination in the 1960s. It was also good for Wall Street bankers and American investors looking to dodge US tax regulation. And it was especially good for the Bahamas. Banking was a lucrative industry that made up an important part of the Bahamian economy, second only to tourism. Pindling and his government understood this. Take away the banking secrecy laws, and you take away the islands' livelihood.

The United States had no qualms about interfering in Bahamian politics. The United States has a long and unfortunate history of doing exactly this sort of thing. Just one example: Guatemala. In the 1950s the United Fruit Company—an American firm that grew and distributed Dole bananas—was the largest landholder in Guatemala. When democratically elected president Jacobo Árbenz Guzmán came to office in 1951, he promised to redistribute land and introduce labor reform. United Fruit panicked and rallied its allies in the Eisenhower White House. The secretary of state was a member of the same law firm that represented United Fruit. The secretary's brother, who was the CIA director, was a board member of the United Fruit Company. Even Eisenhower's personal secretary had a link. Her husband was United Fruit's main lobbyist. The pressure on Eisenhower worked. He put the CIA on the case, and Guzmán was overthrown by a US-backed strongman who had the support of CIA-trained soldiers and US military aircraft. The strongman ruled for the next three years; it was a bloody and brutal regime, the first in a long line of US-supported dictators that led to the Guatemalan Civil War. The war lasted thirty-six years and caused two hundred thousand deaths or disappearances.

American tactics were, thankfully, far less bloody in the Bahamas. Instead of out-and-out warfare, American strategists attacked Pindling in the press. In September 1983 an unidentified source leaked information to the investigative reporter Brian Ross, then at NBC, accusing Bahamian officials of taking bribes from drug smugglers. Ross said the information came from Justice Department intelligence. He used it as material for a lengthy investigative report titled "A Nation for Sale."

In retaliation, Pindling appeared on NBC's *Today* show, where he faced off against Brian Ross. He called Ross a faker and a fraud. "Name one of your sources," Pindling demanded. "I am only asking you to name one." According to a *New York Times* article, Pindling called the NBC report "a criminally conceived conspiracy against the Bahamas." He insisted that he would go "straight to the top" to identify the source. He even sued NBC over the report, though he eventually dropped the case without settlement or apology from the news station. "This is a complete vindication of our journalism," said NBC News President Michael Gartner in response to the dropped suit.

The NBC report prompted a number of articles, including multiple front-page stories in the *Miami Herald*. My father got a brief mention in one. On a map of the chain of the Bahamas that identified the various smuggling groups and the islands they controlled, the Darby Islands were labeled "Lamar Chester." His name had an asterisk beside it that meant "awaiting trial." My teenage sister, who lived in Miami, saw the article. So did her high school teachers and many of her friends. She called our father, angry and ashamed.

"I can't believe you're doing this," she said.

Our dad pushed back. "You have no right to judge me."

They traded barbs, digging the rift between them deeper.

The series in the *Herald* was written by Carl Hiaasen, then an investigative reporter. "Corruption in the Bahamas has transformed one of the world's idyllic destinations into a dangerous smuggler's paradise," Hiaasen wrote. "The old Bahamas was a place of pearly beaches, tranquil harbors and timeless charm. The new Bahamas is a hard-edged place where everything, and almost everyone, has a price. . . . You can buy an airstrip, or an island. You can buy citizenship. You can buy protection. You can buy justice. . . . Corruption spawned and fueled by American drug millionaires has stained every strata of Bahamas officialdom, from constables to Cabinet ministers. The scandal has enfolded some of those nearest to Prime Minister Lynden Pindling—and Pindling himself."

Yet the articles noted that many people in the Bahamas benefited from the drug trade, and not just at the highest levels. "It's touching tens of thousands of lives, many of whom would be living at a much lower level," a shop owner and former Bahamian Parliament member was quoted as saying in the *Herald* article. A former Bahamian assistant commissioner of police said that in late 1979 he led a secret raid on the island of Bimini, which was heavily involved in the drug trade. While his forces fanned out over the island to make arrests, the assistant commissioner waited in the police station. The phone rang, and he picked it up. The voice on the other end of the line was a local Bahamian, irritated that the police hadn't given them a heads-up on the raid.

"Man," the caller said, not realizing he was talking to the assistant commissioner of police himself, "why you all didn't tell us what was going on?"

When the Bahamian police left the island with those they had arrested, the locals gathered to watch them leave. One by one, the people on shore stooped to pick up rocks. They threw them at the boat—not at the men who had been arrested, but at the police who were taking them away.

"What amazes me is that there were children and grown-ups and elderly people," the assistant commissioner said, "and they were all throwing stones at us."

THE NEWS REPORTS on Pindling had their desired effect. In November 1983, two months after the NBC story ran, Pindling called for a Royal Commission of Inquiry to investigate the accusations made by Ross about drug smuggling in the Bahamas. "We will probably hear some things we want to hear. We will probably hear some things we don't want to hear. And we will probably hear some things we know about but want to hide," Pindling said in a radio address to his nation. "Be that as it may, it will in all probability lead to the betterment and the improvement of the Bahamas in the long run."

The Royal Commission would be made of three men. To avoid any suggestion of tainted authority, Bahamian officials scoured the British Commonwealth for three people of unimpeachable integrity. They chose an attorney, a theologian, and a policeman. The attorney was a white Bahamian with a knighthood who guided the proceedings with a polite and gentlemanly air. The theologian was a bishop, and the only Black member of the commission. He used wry humor and a logical mind to shape his questions. The policeman was a former member of the Royal Canadian Mounted Police. He spoke less than the other two men, but when he did speak, he questioned witnesses with directness.

The three-person commission would hear testimony for thirteen months. Their task was to answer a series of questions: Were members of the Bahamian government being bribed by drug smugglers? Were the Bahamian police doing enough to prevent smuggling? How did drugs flow through the Bahamas en route to the United States? And finally, were new laws needed to discourage trafficking? To answer these questions, the commission subpoenaed more than a hundred witnesses, everyone from convicted drug smugglers to members of parliament.

But they didn't need to subpoena my father. He testified voluntarily.

WHILE THE ROYAL Commission was being assembled in the Bahamas, a man who called himself Morgan Cherry contacted my father. The two men agreed to meet inside the Ionosphere Club at the Atlanta International Airport. My father would later testify about their conversation in front of the Royal Commission. An account of his testimony was reported in newspapers as well as in an internal State Department memo.

According to my father's sworn testimony and newspaper reports, Cherry owned a Virginia-based firm called Justice International, which was a registered lobbyist for the Bahamian political party in opposition to the Pindling government. Justice International was located near CIA headquarters, and my father said in his testimony that he believed Cherry to be a contract agent for the CIA.

In their meeting, my father asked Cherry if Cherry was responsible for giving NBC's Brian Ross the DEA NADDIS reports that were the basis for the NBC broadcast.

"You liked that, did you?" Cherry reportedly said.

According to my father, Cherry went on to confirm that, yes, he was the one who passed along the Justice Department documents.

But more than that—and, more importantly, for my father—Cherry had requested the meeting at the Ionosphere Club in order to secure my father's silence. My father later testified that Cherry proposed to have the federal indictment against him dismissed if my father would decline to speak in front of the Royal Commission.

Though he had everything to gain by cooperating with Cherry, my father refused. He later told the commission that he expected "to suffer greatly" for his testimony, but that he did not like to see the US government "messing with another country's politics."

After the meeting at the Ionosphere, my father drove back to the farm in North Georgia and called his attorney, Jeffrey Bogart.

"I need to get to the Bahamas," he told Bogart.

"I'll talk to the judge," his attorney said.

To everyone's surprise, the judge granted my father a special dispensation. He was given his passport, and he made plans to fly to Nassau to testify in front of the Royal Commission.

ON A MUGGY Wednesday morning in May 1984, a light breeze traveled down one of the main thoroughfares of Nassau. The fronds on the royal palms that lined the boulevard made a gentle *shush-shush* as they moved in the breeze. The sky was a pale blue, dotted here and there with puffs of white clouds. This part of the Bahamian capital was far away from the tourist beaches with their smells of coconut oil and sunscreen, their relaxed vibe of vacation insouciance. This was a different Nassau, a grittier Nassau, gray and covered in concrete. The taxis never brought the tourists here on their way from the airport to the hotel. The cruise ships never passed by this section on their tours. This Nassau was for locals only.

The Royal Commission held its hearings inside a former bank building, a single-story utilitarian structure more like a high school cafeteria than a stately government building. On this particular Wednesday, a procession of notable attorneys pulled up outside. Sir Edward Gardner, one of London's most prestigious attorneys and a member of the British House of Lords, arrived in a black limousine. F. Lee Bailey, one of the most prominent lawyers in America at the time, and Robert Ellicott, a former solicitor general of Australia, both followed. They were all there to represent members of the Bahamian government.

Bahamian spectators gathered on the steps of the bank to watch the procession. Old men, out-of-work men, housewives, and market women, all of them dressed in their best clothes, pressed and neatly starched, as if they were going to church. They waited in line, hoping to grab a seat inside the hearing room. And if not, they were content to gossip outside the building until they could get an update during recess. The Royal Commission of Inquiry made for great theater. In the press, in the spectator seats, across the islands, it was the biggest event to happen in the Bahamas since independence. One of the spectators turned to the American reporter beside him. "Your Watergate was nothing compared to this," he said. It was a good scandal, the kind whose juicy tidbits would make fodder for daily conversation in the months to come. Pindling was a revered figure, but many Bahamians also knew there was truth to the whispers about Pindling and drug smugglers.

A small window at the back of the hearing room looked out on an empty parking lot. The window had once been the bank's drive-up teller window. It let in a low, watery light. At the front of the room, the evidence was stored in four cardboard boxes. My father was out on bond, and he was there as a free man, but not all of the witnesses were free. The ones who were prisoners, trading their testimony in exchange for reduced sentences, waited to testify in the bank's vault.

The Australian former solicitor general Robert Ellicott served as chief counsel during the proceedings. A balding man with great bushy eyebrows, Ellicott knew how to appeal to the gallery. He'd sometimes turn from the witness stand to wink at spectators. My father spent two and a half hours on the stand that day. The dialogue between him and Ellicott sounds like a high-stakes cat-and-mouse game of verbal sparring. My father seems to be having fun. "I don't think it's possible the prosecutors in Atlanta could be any tougher than Mr. Ellicott," he told his attorneys later that day. "I certainly hope they aren't. The man is excellent."

In front of the commission, my father freely admitted to drug smuggling. He had been granted immunity in the Bahamas in exchange for his testimony, perhaps as part of a larger calculation, a plan to flee to the Bahamas and continue his life there. He was more closemouthed about his investments, specifically the Darby Islands. Because of the strict banking secrecy laws in the Bahamas, it was impossible to find out who owned Caribe Shores, the investment group that was the registered owner of the Darby Islands. When Ellicott asked my father about it, Lamar swore that he was just a front man for Caribe Shores.

"I do not know where the ownership of the Darby Islands lies," he said.

A frustrated Ellicott railed, "It is astounding that it is not possible for this Commission, with all the powers it has within the Bahamas, to find out who owns Little Darby Island, an important cay."

"If that's astounding, you certainly should understand that I don't know who owns the island either," Lamar said.

"You can't have an agreement unless there are partners to it," Ellicott pressed.

"That doesn't mean they have to be known to one another," Lamar countered.

"What would it take to become a member of this group?" Ellicott asked.

"Got any money?" Lamar said.

The spectators in the gallery tittered.

Lamar continued. "If you were an investor who came to me and wanted to invest some money, I have a variety of investment opportunities that not a person in the world, I think, would raise an eyebrow at, and I'm sure you could make very generous returns on your money. If you want to give me a million dollars, I'll give you two million dollars next year. I'll guarantee it."

Ellicott raised his bushy eyebrows. "Now, how can you guarantee that?"

"I just guarantee it," Lamar said. "You'll have to take my word and not ask me what I do with it."

"Does that mean that it could be used in some sort of illicit activity?"

"It could be," Lamar said. "You are not to ask."

"Not to ask?"

"I would advise you to pay your income taxes on the million you earn."

"The income tax service doesn't care where you got your income from, does it?"

Lamar shook his head. "As I said before, not even if you kill little babies, not in the United States."

At this point, Lamar's attorney, Jeffrey Bogart, broke into the line of questioning.

"We have an expression in the United States called badgering the witness," he said, "and that is what Mr. Ellicott is doing."

Ellicott turned away with a huff. "As Mr. Chester's attorney seems to have taken over the role of witness, I will ask no further questions," he said, sitting down.

Ellicott turned over questioning to other counsel. It was F. Lee Bailey, the prime minister's attorney, who asked my father about his meeting at the Ionosphere Club, the one with Morgan Cherry.

"Did Mr. Cherry indicate to you that he had the power to cause this indictment to be dismissed short of verdict at some time, if you cooperated?" Bailey asked.

"Unequivocally," my father answered.

Cherry did not appear to comment on my father's statements, in the press or in front of the commission, though Kendal Isaacs, leader of the Bahamian opposition, said in his testimony in front of the commission that his party hired Justice International in October 1983, after the NBC broadcast, to raise funds for the opposition. This was according to an internal State Department memo.

IN THE END, Pindling was cleared on all charges, though the commission was divided on whether $3.5 million deposited into the prime minister's accounts came from drug-related activities. Bishop Drexel Gomez, who was part of the three-member commission, wrote the dissenting opinion in his minority report on the prime minister's finances. "It is certainly feasible that all of these payments could have been made from non-drug related sources," Gomez wrote. "But in my opinion, the circumstances raise great suspicion, and I find it impossible to say that the payments were all non-drug related."

Nevertheless, Pindling retained the support of his people. In 1987, three years after the Royal Commission, he won another seat as prime minister.

But the Internal Revenue Service of the United States eventually got what it wanted, though it had to wait another ten years. Pindling was finally voted out of office in 1992, and the new prime minister and his party were much more open to relaxing the country's banking secrecy laws. Following intense pressure from the US government, the Bahamas finally relented. In 2004 it signed a tax and information exchange agreement with the United States. Going forward, the two nations would share banking information on both criminal and civil matters. But by then of course, my father would have been long gone.

18

The Arrest

IN THE WAKE OF THE Bahamian Royal Commission of Inquiry, and under pressure from the US government, the Bahamas began to crack down on smuggling through the islands. Bahamian forces worked in conjunction with the DEA to further the War on Drugs. Though my father had stopped his smuggling operations, the Darby Islands still needed attention. Captain Jack had to be paid. A shipment of fuel was coming in and needed to be signed for. A part for the generator was arriving on the mail boat. With my father stuck in the United States without a passport, my mother had to fly down to Darby. She flew commercial to Georgetown, on Grand Exuma, and then took a boat to Little Darby. On this trip she brought her friend Corinne, a woman she knew from Cleveland who was a frequent visitor at our house. Corinne was one of the many people I knew and loved in North Georgia. My mom brought me, too. One late morning during our trip, Terrel and I were in the main house, playing as we always did. The shortwave radio in the corner crackled with voices between the nearby islands. Corinne lounged on the concrete deck attached to the main house, overlooking the runway. Millie was in the kitchen cleaning up from breakfast, and Captain Jack was sitting with my mom at the bar, making a list of what needed to be done on the island.

They heard the helicopter before they saw it. The DEA and Bahamian forces had started performing regular fly-bys, but this time the sound of rotor blades didn't fade after the initial pass. Instead, the noise got louder. Millie called out from the kitchen.

"There's a boat tying up at the dock," she said. "Bahamian police."

Captain Jack and my mom stood at the same time. They walked out to the deck. Corinne sat up. Millie joined them outside, drying her hands on a dish towel. Terrel and I came, too. We all watched as the helicopter made tight circles over the runway.

"I think they're going to land," Jack said to my mom.

Terrel and I hid behind Millie's legs. A few minutes later, we peeked out to watch as men in camouflage moved toward the house. Twenty-odd policemen were making their way up the runway, machine guns slung over their shoulders.

The main force of officers waited in the hangar while the group's leader and four men came up the stairs. Millie took Terrel and me to the back side of the house to shield us from what was happening. In the main room, the leader spoke gruffly to my mother.

"We're going to search the house," he told her.

"Go ahead," she said.

He pointed to Corinne. "Split them up."

The women were each taken to their separate bedrooms. Millie stayed with us at the back of the house, and Captain Jack watched with his arms crossed as the soldiers rifled through cabinets and pulled up seat cushions. It wasn't long before they found a box of unopened dishes sitting on the kitchen counter. The dishes were clearly new, and they obviously hadn't been declared at a customs checkpoint. A soldier called my mother out from the bedroom to explain.

"Whose dishes are these?" he asked her.

"I don't know," she said.

A lie. They were her dishes. She'd bought them at a department store in Atlanta.

"How can you not know?" the soldier asked. "Isn't this your house?"

"A lot of people come through here," my mother said. "It could have been anyone."

"No duty was paid on these dishes," the soldier pressed.

He was trying to catch her on a technicality, any excuse to take her away.

My mom shrugged. "I don't know what to tell you. They're not my dishes."

The soldier must have realized that the dishes weren't enough to arrest her. Or maybe he was just trying to frighten her. He stalked away, and my mom went back to her bedroom, where she sat and waited.

They turned to Corinne's room next, searching through drawers and under the mattress. They didn't speak as they worked but remained quiet and intimidating. When they'd finished, they ushered Corinne into the master bedroom, where my mom was standing in the middle of the room. They'd found a bag of marijuana hidden in the ceiling.

"Is this yours?" the leader asked.

"No," my mom said. This time, it was the truth.

It wasn't much marijuana, but it was enough to arrest her.

"You'll have to come with us," the soldier said.

My mother had sensed this was coming. "I'll need to change clothes."

"Go ahead," the soldier told her.

The men stayed in the room as she changed out of the terry

cloth romper she'd been wearing. They didn't look away. She dressed in a pair of blue jeans, a T-shirt, and sneakers. Where she was going, she knew, she didn't want to be wearing anything flimsy. She took off her jewelry and handed it to Corinne. She wrote down the name and phone number of their Bahamian attorney and gave it along with cash to her friend. She grabbed a tube of toothpaste. The officers agreed not to put her in handcuffs. She walked back through the main house and said goodbye to me.

"Corinne's going to take you home," she said calmly.

She projected reassurance, but I could feel her fear. I wanted to hold tight to her, to wrap my small arms around her, to keep her close. But I also wanted to be brave so that she would be proud of me. I nodded gravely. I didn't cry.

The soldiers led my mother away, down to the runway, while Jack, Millie, Corinne, Terrel, and I watched from the deck. The helicopter lifted off and slid over the waters of the Exumas toward Nassau.

Corinne hurriedly packed our bags, and Jack got a message over the radio to my father's Bahamian attorney, Nigel Bowe. Bowe arranged for Corinne and me to fly to Nassau the next morning in a private plane that belonged to people who owned a nearby cay. Bowe also called my father, who was prohibited from leaving North Georgia. My dad was irate and—beneath his fury—frightened. He'd been careful to cultivate relationships in the Bahamas by donating generously to both Bahamian political parties. He'd hired Nigel Bowe because Bowe also worked for Pindling. For a long time, this had bought him protection. But now his safe passage had come to an end. My mom and I were collateral damage in the war the US government was waging against my father.

That night I slept in Corinne's room on Darby, confused and afraid, while my mom spent the night in jail, somewhere else I couldn't reach her. Jack took us by boat to the neighboring island the next morning. Corinne held me in her lap. We flew to Nassau, both of us silent the whole way. The Nassau airport was crowded, and I sat quietly on my small suitcase and waited as Corinne stood in line to buy us tickets to Atlanta. She kept nervously glancing at me, afraid that someone would try to abduct me. We had two hours before our flight, and we sat in the airport's restaurant and ate lunch. Fear blanketed us, drew us close together, but kept us silent. My father met our plane at the airport in Atlanta. He held me for a long time after we landed, and I pressed my nose to the crook of his neck and breathed in his feeling of safety.

It had taken Nigel Bowe the rest of that first day and into the night to track down my mother at the Central Jail in Nassau. It was too late for him to reach her at the jail, and she spent the night in the holding cell. The other women there were mostly Haitian market women who'd been arrested for selling fruit without a permit, and at first they gave her a wide berth. Late on the first night, when it was clear to the other women that no one was coming for my mother, they shared their food with her, a handful of sweet bananas.

By the afternoon of the next day, when Bowe was able to get into the jail to see her, he brought her Kentucky Fried Chicken for lunch. When he left, promising to bring her dinner that night, my mom put her hand on his arm.

"Would you bring a couple of big buckets of chicken next time?" she asked.

In the evening he brought enough fried chicken for my mom to share with the other women, who took it and thanked her—but still they wanted nothing to do with the American woman with the fancy Nassau attorney.

Finally, on the third day, Bowe managed to get my mom out of jail. My dad's friend Durbin McCollum flew to Nassau to pick her up. He flew her back to North Georgia, but by now Georgia wasn't any safer than the Bahamas.

19

WITSEC

THAT SUMMER, MY DAD'S BROTHER Tony disappeared. He'd served his two years in prison for the quaalude charges, and afterward he'd moved outside Atlanta with his young son. He and the boy's mother were divorced, and she'd moved away. As part of his plea deal for a reduced sentence on the quaalude charges, Tony had testified in front of the Houston grand juries that had been called in the wake of the Operation Lone Star investigation. Two other witnesses who had testified in front of the same grand juries were now dead. Federal agents were understandably worried, and they pressed Tony to go into the Federal Witness Protection Program. Tony had always told them no. Then one night Tony and my father met at one of their favorite restaurants in Atlanta, a seafood joint beside the airport. Lamar ordered a round of drinks and raw oysters. He waited until the waitress left before he said to Tony in a low voice, "It's time."

"What do you mean, it's time?" Tony asked.

"You have to leave now," Lamar said.

Tony shook his head. "I already told you, I'm not doing it."

My father leaned forward. "A contract's been put on you."

Tony sat dumbfounded while the restaurant bustled around them. My father didn't say who had put the contract on Tony, or how he knew, but Tony guessed it was one of the organized crime families whose money Eisenberg had been washing. Tony slowly nodded his head. He didn't hold it against his brother. He understood that this was the result of choices both of them had made. How could they have known, when they first started flying in a few hundred bales of marijuana, that this was where things would end?

Tony didn't waste time digging into the specifics. Beneath the clatter of silverware, he whispered, "I need to make arrangements. I have an apartment—"

"You don't understand," Lamar said. "You need to leave tonight."

This time, Tony listened. He went back to his apartment and called the Witness Security number. Within twenty minutes, agents were at his door. Tony packed a bag for himself and his little boy, and the two of them were whisked away to a new life.

20

The Courthouse

THAT YEAR, A RARE ECLIPSE darkened the noonday sun, and the farmers around Cleveland talked about what it could mean. It didn't look good for my father, they decided. Still, there was a local groundswell of public opinion supporting my dad. It helped that he was easy to like, plus, let's face it: the folks who lived around Cleveland hated to see the law win.

But make no mistake. The law *was* winning.

Most of the money my dad had made smuggling was tied up in his capital assets—the farm, the Darby Islands, his boats, his planes—and the IRS was making a case to seize them as forfeiture under the federal RICO (Racketeer Influenced and Corrupt Organizations) Act. What cash my dad had left, he was burning through on legal fees. His attorneys had even placed a lien against our house. The world as we knew it was rapidly coming apart.

But I had no idea. I spent that summer playing in the creek beside the house. I fished in the pond down the road. I turned brown as a nut. In June, I was four years old. My dad came with an ice cream truck to the preschool where I spent weekdays. My whole class enjoyed rocket pops, Fudgesicles, and ice cream sandwiches. *Ice cream for everybody! As much as you want!* He brought a go-cart and took the kids for a ride around the parking lot. I stared up at my father, a tall man who was the giver of all things good, the sun around which my world revolved.

Preschool hadn't tamed me. I'd learned that I wasn't supposed to cuss, but it was hard to get me to stop saying "shit." I didn't like playing with the other little girls who wanted to pretend we were keeping house or teaching school. My best friend was a boy with sandy hair, and we spent the afternoons climbing trees and digging in the dirt. I hated that he got to take his shirt off on hot afternoons but I had to keep mine on. Once I defied the rules and threw my shirt over the fence and scampered around like a bare-chested little boy until I got yanked inside and told to put my clothes back on.

My hair grew long and knotted. I wouldn't let anyone put a comb to it. One day my mom took me to the salon and told the woman to cut it off. "All of it," she said. She kept one of the knots as a souvenir, like baby shoes or a first tooth, but the rest of my wild hair ended up on the salon floor. I left there with a pixie cut, looking more like a boy than ever, which suited me just fine.

My sister Jen came to the farm that summer. She was only twelve, but already she was transforming into the tall, slim beauty who would one day model on South Beach. She and our father had called a truce that summer, and my memories of her are pure sweetness. We picked buckets full of blueberries and sat and ate them by the handful while our fingers stained blue. In the evenings, we ran through the grass and caught lightning bugs until long after dark. Then I'd lie on the couch, sleepy and happy, and beg her, "Jen, tickle my back."

The bedroom next to mine was still called Terry's room from when he'd lived on the farm. Sometimes I'd sneak into the room and go through the drawers. The top drawer held the lacy garters he'd caught at weddings, and I thought my brother Terry was impossibly cool. That summer he came to the farm for a visit. He brought his wife, Leigh, and their son, who was two years younger than me. Terry was twenty-four at the time, and I was shy around him, which was unlike me. I hid behind my mom's legs as she tried to coax me out to say hello to my brother. I couldn't manage to speak to this handsome guy who flew airplanes and had a drawer full of garters.

That summer, both sets of my grandparents lived nearby. My dad's pop lived up the hill with his fourth wife. They'd have us over for Sunday breakfast. Pop raised bees, and sometimes he'd put on his bee suit. Other times, he'd take me to feed his donkey, Saint Olaf. He was tall and gruff and reminded me of a storybook giant. I loved him.

My grandparents Art and Jewel were also on the farm that summer. There's a photo of me from this time, a square-shouldered little girl holding a trout. I'm straight-backed, skinny and knob-kneed, wearing a pair of briefs and nothing else. I stand beside my grandpa Art and grin at the fish I'd caught. In other photos from that summer, I'm with my grandma Jewel. Her lips are always pursed with worry. She and my mom spent whole afternoons in the kitchen canning peaches and whispering at the stove while I played with my She-Ra dolls in the living room, oblivious to the trouble swirling around me.

When I think of the perceptive abilities of young children, I imagine the antennae on butterflies, quivering with emotional discoveries invisible to the naked eye. After the crash that killed my father, I quaked with the sensations of disaster that surrounded me. Tragedy and hopelessness radiated from everyone who passed through the house. But when my dad was alive, he was a bulwark against those feelings. His large frame, his confident demeanor, his easygoing charm—all of that served as a talisman against dark forces. He and my mom must have had worried discussions behind closed doors. I'm sure he sat on the porch in the evenings, drinking Bacardi Añejo and ruminating. I know attorneys and reporters came to our house. But I have no memory of any of that. What I remember is my own uncomplicated happiness. My father made me feel safe and protected. With me, he kept the worry that blanketed him at bay, allowing me those short, beautiful years of a briefly charmed life.

AND ALL WAS not lost. Not yet. My father's attorneys had filed a motion to dismiss his case on the grounds of government misconduct, given Frank Robin's bribery attempt and the falsification of evidence revealed by Lesley Bickerton. In August, a hearing on the defense motion was held. My dad's attorney, Bobby Lee Cook, got former assistant US attorney John Johnson in the witness box. The former federal prosecutor from Houston had resigned his post abruptly in 1982, ostensibly because he feared for his life after Bickerton revealed that she'd overheard talk of a contract hit placed on him. Some newspaper articles say Johnson had been forced to resign from the US attorney's office for submitting false travel vouchers and for referring cases to a private law firm. Of course, it's possible that he was forced out because of the mishandling of the Bickerton evidence, though that version of the story has never made it into the public record.

In the courtroom, Johnson sat gripping the sides of the witness box with his hands. He filled the space with his large frame and glared back at Cook as Cook questioned him about Lesley Bickerton and the evidence she'd doctored.

"Now, Mr. Johnson," Cook said. "Part of the documents that she brought over here were either false or, to use the term of the government, added to. Or reconstructed. Are you telling this court today without equivocation and positively that when those documents left Houston to come to Atlanta that you had absolutely no knowledge that the documents were either false, added to, or reconstructed? Is that your testimony?"

"I can say that I had no knowledge that there was anything in those documents that was false, but as to whether they were added to or something was reconstructed, I can't honestly say. And I can't say by who," Johnson replied.

Cook continued. "Did you have any knowledge—had Mr. Friend or Lesley Bickerton or any of the other agents told you before those documents left Houston that they had been tampered with, added onto, reconstructed, and that some of them were false?"

"No. No one told me they were false," Johnson answered.

"You're positive about that?"

"I'm positive."

Though Johnson denied knowing about the reconstructed documents—despite earlier testimony from US customs agent Jeff Friend that Johnson did, in fact, have prior knowledge—what Johnson did not deny was his read on Bickerton.

"I had a sneaking suspicion about her from the first day I met her," Johnson said. "There was something I couldn't put my finger on. She was a double agent, for all I know."

Cook looked at Johnson over the rims of his glasses. "If she was a double agent, then Operation Lone Star was suckered, wasn't it?"

Johnson shifted uneasily. "Well, I don't know," he said. "They probably were."

Cook strode through the courtroom. He paused to glare at Johnson. "She had you all snowed."

Johnson shook his head. "No."

"Is it true," Cook asked, "that a former Justice Department attorney involved in Operation Lone Star had been fired for sleeping with Ms. Bickerton?"

Johnson glanced at the lawyer representing the government. The lawyer didn't say a word.

"That's what I heard," Johnson said.

It was true, according to Bickerton. She claimed in a sworn statement she'd slept with a federal prosecutor named Ferris "Ridge" Bond the night before she appeared in front of the Houston grand jury. Bond had been forced to resign his role as one of the case supervisors.

Cook went on to attack Bickerton's credibility, calling her a "rudderless ship in a high sea." He got US customs agent Jeff Friend to admit on the stand that Bickerton was "not the most stable person."

Eventually, Bickerton took the stand herself. Bobby Lee Cook, who had skewered the other witnesses, treated her with a surprising gentleness. He asked about her dog, the one Bickerton said my brother Terry had stolen from her. She started to cry.

"It was the only thing I ever had in my life," she said.

She sobbed so hard the judge asked if she needed a recess. Bickerton shook her head, no.

"Did the IRS agent promise to help you get your dog back?" he asked.

"Yes, sir," Bickerton said. "He told me that. That was the main reason I told them what I knew about Lamar."

Cook nodded sympathetically. "That was the main motivating factor?"

"Yes, sir."

"And did you later learn that the promise was a lie?"

"I did. That's why I went to Lamar's attorneys."

Cook paused and gave Bickerton a moment to catch her breath before he asked about her interaction with the federal agents.

"It wasn't right—none of it was right," Bickerton said.

She admitted that she feared John Johnson, who was in charge of the case when she was recruited as an informant. "I was afraid I would be hurt. I felt like he didn't have any regard for anybody."

"Or for the truth," Cook said.

"Yes, sir."

"He wanted you to lie."

"Yes, sir."

Bickerton dabbed at her eyes with a tissue.

It's hard to say whether Bickerton's testimony was completely real. Or was some of it performance? One of the reporters covering the case called her one of the most manipulative people he'd ever met. She'd certainly come across as an unreliable witness.

She never did get her dog back. The Doberman died of old age at Terry's house.

THE HEARING ON the motion to dismiss my dad's case spanned eight days. Despite the high tension inside the courtroom, the atmosphere just outside it was convivial. My father was there for each of the days of the hearing. He looked sophisticated in his wire-rimmed glasses and dark suit, as if he might be one of the attorneys. My mom was there, impeccably dressed, and she and my father circulated like the hosts of a glamorous cocktail party, speaking to attorneys and spectators. Their friends came, many of them the codefendants listed on the indictment. Their own trials would be much later. One friend even brought fresh-baked zucchini bread to share with the court during the midmorning coffee break. They formed their own small community inside the federal courthouse.

Some days I went to the courthouse too. My mom would wrestle me into a dress, and I'd sit in the front row of the courtroom, swinging my feet and staring out the big windows at the summer sky. A shadow of worry had begun to cloud my bright childhood. I'd wait quietly until the proceedings had ended for the day, and then I'd crawl into my dad's lap, the place where I felt safest. He'd rock me against his chest as he talked to his attorneys, still hopeful that his case might be dismissed.

21

Summer 1985

MY FATHER SPENT THE FIRST half of 1985 marooned in North Georgia. He'd been forced to surrender his pilot's license as a condition of his bond, but he'd petitioned the court to have it returned so that he could fly to meet his attorneys in Atlanta and Summerville. The court had agreed, though his range was limited. Neither of us knew it, but this time would be a gift. I was almost five years old, the age when memories start to stick. Nearly all of what I remember about my father comes from those last few months of his life.

I remember a long drive on the winding roads that led from the farm up through the mountains. It's early spring, and the day is gray and misted. A dampness has settled over the trees. The windows of my dad's truck are cranked down, and he's singing Willie Nelson. He holds the steering wheel with an easy grip as we bump over the dirt road. "Watch for squirrels," he says to me. "Next time I'll bring the shotgun and teach you how to shoot."

I remember a warm afternoon in late spring. My dad comes up from the hangar where he's been working on one of his planes. I'm waiting for him on the black leather couch at the top of the stairs. He says, "A.J., let's go for a swim." I race after him, and we jump in the pool.

I remember a day in early summer. My dad stops at a roadside stand selling hot boiled peanuts. He gets a paper bag full, and we sit in the dusty cab of his truck. We eat them scalding hot. He teaches me to dig the soft peanut out of the shell with my teeth, and I giggle at my fingertips that wrinkle from the salty brine. Tall pine trees shade the truck, and the air feels warm and green. The radio plays one of my dad's favorite songs, and we sing together at the chorus. *Country roads, take me home* . . .

I remember a hot afternoon in the middle of June, the pine pollen so thick that the air is yellow. My dad asks me if I want to go for a flight in the Piper Cub.

"Yeah, Daddy," I say.

He grabs his aviators and heads toward the hangar.

"Then let's go, baby girl."

PART IV

22

Disappeared

I SURVIVED THE PLANE CRASH that killed my father, with a small dent at my hairline, a metal rod along my spine, and a scar from my surgeries that would make people ask *What happened to your back?* for the rest of my life. But otherwise I was fine.

Of course, *fine* is a relative term.

Though there had been pain at the hospital—endless, excruciating pain—I don't remember pain afterward. What I remember is itching. I had a body cast around my torso for months, and the skin at the incision point on my back made me crazy as it healed. The techs finally had to cut a hole in the cast to give my back some air and let people scratch it for me. Friends and family stayed in our house for a long time after the crash. They'd put me on the ground like a turtle and spin me, and I would laugh and laugh. That's what I remember. But recently I found photos from that time. The little girl in the pictures is pale and shrunken. She's hunched over, her shoulders pulled in, her legs stiff, the bulky cast pushing against her dress. Her skin is ashen, her face stricken. The photo is a study in trauma.

The day I came home from the hospital, the IRS had posted a seizure notice on our front door. Almost everything that belonged to my father—his cars, his planes, his boats, the five hundred acres of My Goal Farm and the house we lived in—would be seized as forfeiture by the US government. The one piece of property the government was not able to take was the Darby Islands. My brother Bill negotiated a lease for the islands, and he'd spend the rest of his life fighting to keep them.

I quickly learned that I wasn't supposed to talk about my dad to anyone, not even my mom. I loved her fiercely, and I knew that talking about him made her sad. I picked up the details about my dad's drug smuggling case from glances at newspapers and whispered conversations between adults. I didn't fully understand the significance of words like *indictment* and *prosecutors*, but I knew that to talk about my dad would make the people around me fall silent. With my childlike understanding, I interpreted these silences to mean that people were ashamed of my father. So he became a shameful secret that I tacitly agreed to hide. Secrecy built up like scar tissue, twisted and knotted. The more time passed, the thicker it became.

AFTER MY DAD died, the people who knew him vanished from my life. The defense motion to dismiss his case on grounds of prosecutorial misconduct was ultimately unsuccessful, even with everything that came out during the pretrial hearings. Rather than risk a trial, all but one of the codefendants listed on the indictment took plea deals, including my brother Terry, who received a sentence of three years. The only one not to take a deal was my dad's best friend, Ron Elliott, who was tried and sentenced to twenty years.

But even the people who did not go to prison were cut out of my life with a surgical precision. In an attempt to hide my dad's business from me, my mom exiled anyone who had to do with drug smuggling, and because my father had recruited from their friends and family, that meant just about everyone we knew. She was protecting us, but she was also isolating us. Our life, which had once been so big, drew down to a very small circle. The people who had filled our house and filled my days, people who had scratched my back and rocked me in their laps, people whom I'd loved—they all disappeared, along with my father. There were just a few exceptions: my brother Bill, who'd become a successful anesthesiologist; my sister Jen, who'd been too young to get involved; and my mom's parents, Art and Jewel. Everyone else was gone.

IT TOOK THE IRS two years to finally seize our house. By that time, the doctors in Atlanta had given my spine the final all-clear. On a blue-sky morning in the summer of 1987, a moving truck parked in front of our house. Movers spent the day loading what was left of our possessions. When the house was empty, my mom and I sat outside on the front porch, looking out over the mountains. My own sadness felt small in comparison to the immensity of her grief. Of course, my grief wasn't small. It was bottomless, but I was learning to compact my feelings tight so that no one could see. That afternoon, a reporter who had known my father well came to the farm to say goodbye. He snapped a few photos. My mom's despair is palpable in the pictures, but not mine. I'm laughing, the perfect image of a light-hearted little girl.

But in the late afternoon I slipped away to the creek near our house, and in that secret spot I let myself cry. My small body shook with the force of it. I cried for all that we had lost and all the loss that was still to come. I wasn't even seven, and I was tiny and fragile and broken. Beside me, a clear stream of cool water trickled over moss-covered stones. Wild muscadines grew on the fence that ran on the far side of the creek. Sunlight filtered down through the leaves. More than anything, I wanted to stay in that place where I had once felt safe and happy and loved. I closed my eyes and wished for all the things I could not have.

THE NEXT MORNING, my mom and I drove to Florida. First to Clewiston, where we stayed with my grandparents, then to the coast, where we lived in the little house on the gulf that my grandpa had put up for my father's bond.

Life looked nothing like when my dad was alive. Everything seemed to erase that earlier history. We had no money. Almost no family or friends. There were no photos of my father anywhere. My mom went back to teaching, and we never talked about our life in North Georgia, though every day I missed our house and the mountains and the clear creek hidden beneath the trees. One day our neighbor from up the mountain called to tell my mom that the farm had been sold to a man who owned a string of quarries. Our house would be torn down and our mountain stripped for gravel. I have not seen my mom cry many times in my life, but that was one of them.

Somewhere in all this, my memories of my father began to slip away. I forgot the way his voice sounded and how his cologne smelled and whether he read to me at night before bed. I forgot holding his hand. I forgot his laugh. I forgot almost everything about him, except for a few brief moments in the plane the day we went down. I remembered sitting forward and asking if we were going to crash. I remembered my father telling me no, to sit back down. But the memories surrounding those few seconds—what came before and what came after—were lost to me. I struggled to get them back, to piece together what happened that day, but it was as if they had simply been erased. I was the only surviving witness to my father's death, the one person who held the key to understanding the crash, and I couldn't remember what happened. I had failed him.

EVENTUALLY, I STARTED to believe that my mom was right. The only way forward was to leave our old life behind. I became a bookish, studious kid. Education was my way of distancing myself from what I understood to be my father's shame. I worked hard in high school with one goal, to attend a prestigious college far away from the world where I had grown up. But soon after I was accepted to an Ivy League university, I realized my mistake. A fancy school wouldn't be enough to erase the shame I carried. The kids at my college moved through their universe with a confidence I would have killed for. I didn't possess one drop of it, but what I did have was the hidden suspicion that my father had once been somebody important, a man other people respected, someone who had controlled large sums of money. But money, I quickly learned in that world of privilege, wasn't everything. In one of my college seminars, the professor asked, "How do we define class?" and though I was never a hand-raiser, I was sure of the right answer. "It's money," I blurted out, "and the things you can buy with it." The professor shook her head. "No, class isn't money. A drug dealer makes more money than a schoolteacher, but I'd argue that the schoolteacher has more class." I sat there, too stunned to respond. Had she seen it on me, somehow, my connection to the drug trade? My father was a smuggler, not a dealer, yet in terms of class, I suppose he was still at the bottom. *We* were still at the bottom.

I moved through that elite university taking up little space.

Researchers say kids have an uncanny ability to sniff out class. Children in the same elementary school will invariably pair up with other students whose parents share the same or similar professions. Who in that college could be like me? Who had come from two poor parents who had briefly known the kind of wealth that had politicians scraping and bowing, whose influence extended to US senators and foreign prime ministers, and who then had lost it all? I'd been rich for five years, and poor far longer. Of course, I have no doubt that many of the other students' parents engaged in illegal activities. This was the Enron era, after all. Swindling of all kinds paid for these educations. But white-collar swindling is different from trafficking in narcotics. I understood that. I could feel it everywhere, in every ounce of learned privilege that surrounded me.

People talked a lot about their fathers at that university. The father who was a diplomat. The father who was a CEO. I got in the habit of answering questions about my father swiftly and dismissively. "He was a pilot for Eastern," I'd tell anyone who asked. "He died a long time ago." If they pressed, wanting to know how my dad died, I'd say, "A plane crash." They'd look at me with eyes wide, and I'd have to add, "It was a private plane." The follow-up question was always the same. "Was anyone else hurt?" I'd have to say, "I was in the plane, too. I broke my back." Then I'd change the subject.

I hated talking about the plane crash. I hated remembering it. I hated reliving it. I hated the feelings that washed over me as I thought about being lifted out of the plane, a combination of pain and fear and helplessness and rage. But for most people, it's the most important part of my dad's story.

I CARRIED THE secrecy that surrounded my father for thirty years. Eventually, I grew weary from the weight of it. I was thirty-five years old when I began researching this story. I was no longer married. I did not have children. I lived in a cottage in Florida with two cats and a lot of plants. I felt endlessly, unfathomably alone. The low-grade depression that I'd lived with for most of my life had flared into something much harder to manage. I was spiraling into a frightening place.

In his work on trauma, *The Body Keeps the Score*, psychiatrist Bessel van der Kolk writes that there is a heavy cost for keeping traumatic memories at bay. Often those who are unable to integrate their trauma are doomed to repeat it, over and over, as a way of reliving but not processing the experience. I'd never processed my father's death or the plane crash that killed him or the way he disappeared from my life. Instead, I'd spent thirty years living in silence and shame, pulled between my love for my father and the way the world saw him as a smuggler and a criminal.

Unprocessed trauma affects people in different ways. For me, it was slowly eroding my ability to connect. I had begun shutting myself off from the world, and the interactions that came easily to most—marriage, children, coworkers, friends—were becoming impossible for me to navigate. More than anything, I wanted to reach out and find myself held, not by a single person but by an entire network of people who loved and fought and bled together, whose roots were as long and extensive as those of the giant oak that grew in my backyard, people I could call family.

Late at night in my little house in Florida, with the sound of tree frogs echoing against the windows, I'd scroll through videos on my phone. For a while my feed was funny cat videos and skin-care advice and endless tutorials on how to grow houseplants. Then it was therapists and life coaches and tarot readers. Eventually, my feed had only one theme: how to change your life. That's when my father's story began to call out to me, promising an escape from the dark place into which I'd fallen. His story wasn't just about him. It was also about me. Uncovering it would mean facing the shame I'd perceived around him most of my life, as well as the shame I'd imagined in me. It was a way to own the parts of myself that I'd been putting my hand over and hiding for years. I'd have to let go of the pieces that I'd thought would make me whole—a good education, a respectable job, a tidy house in a nice neighborhood—and finally acknowledge the truth: I am my father's daughter, rough and strong-willed, a mix of both the high and the low, the good and the bad. But to do this, I'd have to do the one thing that was hardest for me, something that had become nearly impossible. I'd have to reach out.

IT TOOK ME a long time to work up the nerve to talk to my mom about my dad, even though we've always been close. My mom is the first person I go to when I want to celebrate good news or commiserate over bad news. She is a good listener, and she's always on my side. But despite everything I've shared with her over the years, she still remains very private. She swears she's never been in a relationship since my dad died. I've never seen her go on a date. She is, I believe, still very much in love with him. How hard it must have been for her to turn her back on him and the memories of their life together for the sake of protecting us.

My mom worked as a teacher for thirty years before she retired. She's had a series of cats over the years, strays that she's loved tenderly. She raises butterflies in screen enclosures in her garage and releases them once they emerge from their chrysalides. Her yard is filled with monarchs that flit through her tropical plants. She lets her guard down with animals, softening the hard shell that she's drawn around herself. She loves growing things, though she prefers the scrubby Florida natives that do well in her sandy soil over the fragile hibiscuses and orchids sold in nurseries. For many years after my dad died, she never cut her hair. She stopped wearing makeup and pretty clothes and silver bangles on her wrists. Her outward self began to mirror her tough, impenetrable interior. She was done chasing the high life.

Despite her hard exterior, my mom has a good circle of friends. She's likable, and people want to be around her. But she never lets anyone too close. Including me. Yet if I was going to understand my father, I'd need to scale the wall of secrecy that we had built together.

On my thirty-fifth birthday, I sat across from her at a table in a nice restaurant, working up the courage to bring up my father. My mom looked like an older version of her younger self—her hair was still long and parted in the middle. She'd let it go gray naturally, but much of it was still dark. Her cheekbones were high and defined, her green eyes bright. Her skin was lined and tanned from working outside in her yard. She didn't wear mascara or eyeshadow or blush or lipstick. She had small gold hoops in her ears and an inexpensive watch on her wrist. We ordered two glasses of champagne in honor of my birthday. My mom is not a drinker, and champagne always hits her hard. I waited until she'd gotten nearly to the end of her first glass before I said, "I want to talk about Dad."

In my entire adult life, I'd never said those words.

My mom took a slow sip of champagne. "What do you want to talk about?"

"The business," I said.

My mom gave me a wary look. "The business?"

"The drug smuggling business."

She sat back and pressed her hand to her heart. "You know?"

"I've always known."

"All these years, I've tried to keep it from you," she said.

"I know," I told her.

She took the last swallow of her champagne and set down the glass. "So, what do you want me to tell you?"

"All of it," I said.

My mom looked at the table and then back up at me. "Well, let's talk."

23

Uncle Tony

IN THE SPRING OF 2019, I got on a plane to visit my uncle Tony. I'd like to tell you where I was headed—north toward the towering maples of the Atlantic seaboard, their branches still bare in the cool spring air; or west toward the desert, a dry and sandy place of cacti and agave; or to the middle of the country, where snow still blanketed the flat plains. But I can't reveal any of those details. Tony is still in the Federal Witness Protection Program. He's had to pick up and move twice since he went into witness protection in 1984, both times leaving behind one life and taking on another with less than twenty-four hours' notice. He still has the WITSEC number taped to his fridge. If his location is compromised, he'll call the number and disappear before morning. He decided to trust me, he said, because I was Lamar's daughter.

Tony was seventy-three when we met. He had a nice, quiet life that he didn't want to uproot. I had a quiet life too. But sometimes we have to uproot everything.

By the time I visited Tony, I had become someone I no longer recognized, a shadow of the person I had once been. When I was twenty-six years old, I was married. My husband, like my father, was a pilot. He flew helicopters in the army. Three weeks after our wedding, he deployed to Iraq. Four months later, his helicopter crashed in a lemon orchard outside Balad. They tell me he died instantly.

My husband's death was like a terrible storm. It came in and wiped me out, down to the concrete slabs. If I hadn't lost my father in a similar way, then perhaps I would have been able to rebuild my life after my husband died. But two traumas of that magnitude, separated by twenty years, made it impossible. So I re-created a semblance of a life—a good life, even. I went to graduate school, I became a journalist, I reported in West Africa. I lived in New York. I sold my first book. I traveled widely. I had friends and lovers. But the life I was craving, a life filled with deep connections? No. I rebuilt what I could using pieces of corrugated tin, scraps of lumber, a blue tarp for a roof. I pulled this shelter over myself, and I waited for the next storm, the one that would come in and wipe it all away again.

TONY AND I had talked on the phone a lot by this point—hours and hours—but I hadn't seen him since before my dad's death, when I was still a little girl. Yet the fact remained: he's my uncle. He may have done time in prison, and he may have testified against people I loved, but he was my dad's brother. If I was ever going to understand my dad's story, I'd have to stand close to the people who knew him. I needed to meet his family. *My* family.

One of the first things Tony told me when the Uber dropped me off from the airport was "I drink bourbon on the rocks." It was after 10:00 p.m., and he was wearing lounge pants and a Panama Canal T-shirt. He had a glass of Maker's Mark in his hand. The ice rattled as he talked. He was tall, lanky, and broad-shouldered, with a full head of white hair. He wore slippers and a pair of rose-tinted John Lennon glasses. He had a gold ring on his left pinkie. His Pomeranian, Elly, pranced around my feet until I sat on the carpet and scratched behind her ears. She wheezed and snuffled while Tony and I made chitchat.

The day had been long, and it was late. Tony offered to show me to my room and I followed, relieved. Like the rest of the house, the guest room was well cared for and immaculately clean. There were thoughtful touches like a basket of soap and shampoo on the dresser, clean towels and a washcloth neatly folded on the foot of the bed. Tony left me to settle in, and I looked at the books on the shelf against one wall. My dad's favorite's book, *Jonathan Livingston Seagull*, was lying on its side. I picked it up and paged through the book. It felt right, like a sign that everything would be OK. I was awash in the strangeness and beauty of life when Tony knocked on the door.

"You want to see the Milky Way?" he asked.

"I'd love to," I said.

I followed him outside, and we stood in front of the house, craning our necks. The air was cool and clear. The stars were vibrant pinpricks against the black sky. Tony, beside me, was uncannily familiar. I thought of everything I'd heard about family—blood is thicker than water and all that—and for the first time I understood what it meant. Tony wasn't a stranger to me. Sure, I hadn't seen him in more than three decades, but I felt it as clearly as I saw the Milky Way overhead, bright and inexorable. We're family.

IN THE MORNING, we got down to business. Tony was up early. He'd dressed in plaid pajama pants and a black ZZ Top T-shirt. He had on his rose-tinted glasses. His slippers slapped against the polished tiles of the kitchen floor as he moved, shifting pots and pans. He pulled a package of sausages out of the fridge and set to frying them in a skillet, talking the whole time. He told me about my dad bringing my mom a pineapple on their first date. He described the restaurant where my dad told him he needed to go into witness protection. He talked about Jeffrey Bogart and Lance Eisenberg and Sibley Riggs. He told me the story about my father's crash in the Everglades, about Vera's broken wrist, about the two stories that branched from that crash—the one where my father was the hero, and the one where he was not. He told me my father was more cautious about fuel after that.

Tony walked to the fridge and took out a handful of frozen green beans. "She loves these," he said, stooping to give Elly a snack. When he stood, he asked, "How's your mother?"

"She's good," I said.

He seemed to be waiting for more, so I added, "I didn't tell her I'm here."

He nodded. "Probably better that way."

He started to turn toward the stove but stopped. "You know, I have a copy of the National Transportation Safety Board report on your dad's crash."

My breath caught in my throat. I'd never seen the report.

Tony walked to his computer desk in the living room and came back with the printed report. He read the date and time of the crash out loud. June 20, 1985, 6:15 p.m.

"Your dad always liked to fly in the evenings when it cooled down," he said.

He handed me the report, and I sat at the breakfast bar and read it while Tony moved around the kitchen, opening cupboards, taking out pots and pans.

ANALYSIS: THE PLT TOOK OFF FROM A PRIVATE STRIP WITH HIS 5 YR OLD DAUGHTER ON BOARD. HE THEN MADE SEVERAL LOW PASSES BY A GUEST HOUSE SO THAT HIS DAUGHTER COULD WAVE TO HER GRANDPARENTS. THE ACFT WAS LAST SEEN HEADED GENERALLY IN A NORTHERLY DIRECTION WHEN IT BANKED SHARPLY TO THE RIGHT, THEN IT DISAPPEARED BEHIND TREES. IMPACT OCCURRED IN A STEEP NOSE-DOWN ATTITUDE. THERE WAS AN ABSENCE OF TORSIONAL DAMAGE TO THE PROPELLER; ONE BLADE WAS STRAIGHT & THE OTHER BLADE WAS BENT AFT. VIRTUALLY NO FUEL WAS FOUND IN THE TANKS, LINES & CARBURETOR. NO PREIMPACT PART FAILURE OR MALFUNCTION WAS FND. DURING AN OPERATIONAL CHECK WITH A REPLACEMENT PROPELLER, THE ENG WAS RUN TO 2325 RPM. A CHECK OF THE PLT'S BLOOD SHOWED AN ALCOHOL LVL OF 0.040%.

Under the heading "Probable Cause and Findings":

Occurrence #1: LOSS OF ENGINE POWER (TOTAL)— NONMECHANICAL

Phase of Operation: MANEUVERING
1. (C) AIRCRAFT PREFLIGHT—INADEQUATE—PILOT IN COMMAND
2. (F) IMPAIRMENT (ALCOHOL)—PILOT IN COMMAND
3. (C) FLUID, FUEL—EXHAUSTION
4. (C) FUEL SUPPLY—INADEQUATE—PILOT IN COMMAND
5. (F) DIVERTED ATTENTION—PILOT IN COMMAND

Occurrence #2: FORCED LANDING

Phase of Operation: MANEUVERING—TURN TO LANDING AREA (EMERGENCY)

Occurrence #3: LOSS OF CONTROL—IN FLIGHT

Phase of Operation: MANEUVERING—TURN TO LANDING AREA (EMERGENCY)

Findings
1. (F) TERRAIN CONDITION—HIGH OBSTRUCTION(S)
2. (C) AIRSPEED—NOT MAINTAINED—PILOT IN COMMAND
3. (C) STALL—INADVERTENT—PILOT IN COMMAND

Occurrence #4: IN FLIGHT COLLISION WITH TERRAIN/WATER

Phase of Operation: DESCENT—UNCONTROLLED

The report's conclusion was simple. My father had alcohol in his system. Probably two drinks based on his weight and the 0.040% blood alcohol level. He'd inadequately preflighted the airplane, meaning he didn't check whether or not he had gas in the tank before he took off. Over the course of our short flight, the plane ran out of fuel. This had caused the Piper Cub to lose airspeed and go into a stall. The plane fell in an uncontrolled descent and collided with the ground.

By now, Tony was at the stove with his back to me, making sausage gravy.

"They said it was fuel starvation," he said, "that the plane ran out of fuel. But there was a small fire, so there had to have been some fuel."

I thought of my grandpa Art pulling me out of the plane, the way he said afterward that he smelled gas. Gas everywhere.

"A Piper Cub can fly at thirty miles an hour and glide pretty good without gas," Tony said. "Even if Lamar had run out of fuel, I know he could have landed that plane."

I thought of all the stories I'd heard about my dad always having a landing spot in mind.

Tony had taken a can of biscuits out of the fridge, and he cracked it open on the kitchen counter. "From the early stages, we suspected the government killed Lamar. Almost immediately."

I tried to keep the shock from my face. Was I hearing him right? If I was, then Tony was saying that the story I'd believed my entire life might not be the whole truth.

"Who in the government would have wanted to kill my dad?" I asked.

Tony shrugged. "DEA. CIA."

"But why would they want to kill him? They had been about to put him on trial. Surely that would be all the win they needed."

Tony turned to the kitchen counter and began carefully laying the biscuits out on the baking sheet. "Because he was threatening to expose all their secrets."

For Tony, this was a story he'd lived with for more than thirty years. But for me, it was all brand-new. I sat at the kitchen counter reeling while my uncle finished making us breakfast. The plane crash—*the accident*—was no accident at all, according to Tony. Everything I knew, or thought I knew, was suddenly upended.

24

Covert Agent

IN JANUARY 1984, ATLANTA'S WAGA-TV ran a three-part series about my father. Forrest Sawyer, then a young newsman in Atlanta, came to the farm to interview my dad. My father never denied being a drug smuggler. In fact, he told Sawyer that he had flown at least two hundred loads of marijuana into the United States. But he claimed to be doing it with the full knowledge—and blessing—of the federal government.

My sister Jen was at the farm the day of the interview. Her flight back to Miami was that evening, and our dad asked Sawyer to give her a ride to the airport. During the drive to Atlanta, my sister asked Sawyer what it meant that our dad said he was working with the federal government. "I think Lamar has gotten involved in something much bigger than him," Sawyer said.

MY FATHER WASN'T just talking to reporters. During his testimony in front of the Bahamian Royal Commission, he'd claimed that he worked for both Customs and DEA as a freelance operative. He testified in great detail about his covert work. He told the commission that an officer for US Customs asked him to get an Eastern Airlines pilot out of jail in the Bahamas. The pilot was there on a smuggling conviction, and the Bahamian government was refusing to extradite him. US agencies wanted the pilot back, most likely because he was an informant.

"The agent said if I had to break him out, to take him to Mexico," my father testified. "Then they would take him from there."

The attorney for the prime minister nodded. "Did the customs agent specify a preference as to whether to break him out of Fox Hill prison or buy his way out?"

"No, they didn't," Lamar said.

The attorney questioned him about a second case, one where my father was hired to bring an American smuggler at large in the Bahamas back to the United States. My father didn't say why the feds wanted this man captured, but it's easy to believe that—like the Eastern Airlines pilot in the Bahamian jail and like my father himself—he was another cog in the War on Drugs machine. The attorney for the prime minister asked how my father would pull off the man's capture. "You would invite him aboard your airplane and then go to quite a different destination than he had expected?"

"They just wanted to get him back in the country," Lamar said, "so I suggested that I fly him directly to Homestead Air Force Base, leave him handcuffed to the runway lights, and they could come out and get him."

THE US GOVERNMENT itself was also talking about my father's work for them. In the fall of 1983, the House Committee on Foreign Affairs held a series of hearings on drug smuggling in the Bahamas. Bahamian leaders were insisting that US agencies were conducting secret operations there, without the permission of the Bahamian government, in violation of international laws. The head of the subcommittee, Ohio representative Edward Feighan, was particularly interested in my father's ongoing case. At the

October 19 hearing, Representative Feighan addressed an agent from the DEA:

> Congressman: If I could ask you some questions with regard to your agency's activities, one of the disturbing things surrounding all of our discussions about drug trafficking through the Bahamas have been some of the news allegations, some of which have been directed against Bahamian officials. I do not see it within the purview of this committee to really investigate these particular allegations, but I do think we have to be very concerned about allegations against our own departments and the activities that our departments and agencies engage in. And some Bahamian officials, including the Prime Minister, have charged that in some instances we have been acting in an illegal fashion in the conduct of our narcotics control efforts in the Bahamas. Recently there was an indictment of several individuals—one Tilton Lamar Chester—I think you know who I am referring to.
>
> DEA: I know who that is; yes.
>
> Congressman: And we have seen news reports of Mr. Chester, that he has been operating as an agent of DEA. I wonder if you might take this occasion to comment on that and tell us to what extent, if at all, Mr. Chester has been an agent for the DEA.

DEA: Congressman, as a matter of policy, I could not comment on any individual, if you are referring to an individual, acting as an informant for the DEA. It is our policy not to disclose the names of informants.

Congressman: I would only ask you to clarify that. I was not asking as respect to his role as an informant but as an agent.

DEA: He has never been an agent of the DEA. I can state that unequivocally. I did see a news article, as I recall; there was an article that referred to the fact that he said he had flown DEA agents around the Bahamas. I believe that was the statement, and I believe the year was 1981, if I am not mistaken. And I have looked into that, and I can find no reference to that in any of our files. It is not a factual statement. Let me just reaffirm that I am correct. The article, and I do not remember where it appeared, was brought to my attention, and it was without foundation as far as I know. But I would not normally disclose an individual's cooperation no matter who that individual was. I hope the committee can appreciate that.

Congressman: Certainly, I can. This is an individual who stands under indictment on several charges.

DEA: Most of the people who cooperate with us do stand under indictment.

Congressman: He was only recently indicted. Are you suggesting that most of the people who work with you end up under indictment?

DEA: No, sir.

Congressman: I just wanted to make sure we clarified that. I have a copy of a letter from Mr. Roger Olson, the Deputy Assistant General. He is corresponding with Mr. Chester's attorney, and he says in that letter, on Department of Justice's letterhead: "We have learned of contacts between your client, Tilton Lamar Chester, and special agents of the Drug Enforcement Administration." This is the Justice Department talking about those contacts. "This is to advise you that all such contacts are independent of the Atlanta grand jury investigation of your client. Whatever understanding or agreement your client may reach or believes he may have reached with the Drug Enforcement Administration, all decisions with respect to the Atlanta investigation and its ultimate outcome can only be made by the United States attorney." Et cetera. What kind of contacts has Tilton Lamar Chester had with DEA?

DEA: Well, I would not go into specifics, Congressman, but it is not unusual for people who are under indictment, or feel that they are about to be indicted, to contact a law enforcement agency in an attempt to help themselves in this situation. I would prefer not to comment on the specifics of this particular case, but that is not an unusual circumstance for any individual who is under indictment or feels that he might be under indictment.

In other words, the DEA was willing to admit that my father might have been an informant, but it was definitely not willing to admit that he was working for the agency as a covert operative.

What strikes me in this conversation is its muddiness, how the DEA officer refused to "go into specifics" and used the type of language that some might call deflecting language—"As far as I know" and "I can find no reference to that in any of our files." It's impossible for me to read this exchange without thinking about the kind of manipulation the US government has been accused of for decades, on both the micro and macro level. On the micro level, it points to affecting a single person's life: my father, who was caught in the bigger political maneuverings of US policies at the time—drug policy and also nation-building. By absolving the DEA of any knowledge or connection to my father, the agency could simply wipe its hands clean of the story. Whatever Lamar Chester had done for the US government would remain hidden from public scrutiny. He would become just another dope smuggler destined to do hard time. That would have worked out well for everybody. Everybody in the government, at least.

On the macro level, this hearing touches on just one of the many allegations of US interference in the governments of sovereign nations. In this instance, they're discussing the Bahamas.

But throughout this nation's history, any number of countries could be substituted in the conversation—Iraq, Afghanistan, Vietnam, Chile, Cuba, Panama, Guatemala, Nicaragua. This intentionally vague testimony from a minor DEA officer at the tail end of a congressional panel, its members clamoring to call it a day, is merely a minor blip in a long history of US government obfuscation.

TO UNDERSTAND THE truth about my father's work for the federal government, I started filing Freedom of Information Act requests. I reached out to three US agencies—the CIA, the FBI, and the DEA. I said I was looking for information about Tilton Lamar Chester Jr. I didn't mention drug smuggling or covert operations. I simply gave his name, his date of birth, his date of death, and his Social Security number. I said I was his daughter.

The CIA was the first to get back to me. This was the agency's response:

> After conducting a search reasonably calculated to uncover all relevant documents, we did not locate any responsive records that would reveal a publicly acknowledged CIA affiliation with the subject.

OK, I thought. Tony had gotten it wrong. There was no CIA connection. But then I paused. Where my father's story is concerned, I've learned to look at the negative spaces. I try to hear what's not being said. The letter went on:

> To the extent that your request also seeks records that would reveal a classified association between the CIA and the

subject, if any exist, we can neither confirm nor deny having such records. . . . If a classified association between the subject and this organization were to exist, records revealing such a relationship would be properly classified and require continued safeguards against unauthorized disclosure. You may consider this finding a denial of this portion of your request pursuant to FOIA exemptions . . .

We can neither confirm nor deny having such records. What did that mean?

I turned to the internet for more information. I wanted to know if this was the CIA's standard response. Did everyone who put in a FOIA request with the agency receive the same "neither confirm nor deny" letter? The answer is no. This particular letter is what's known in FOIA circles as the Glomar response. It uses the neither-confirm-nor-deny clause to skirt the agency's disclosure requirements under the Freedom of Information Act. The term itself originated with the name of a boat, the *Glomar Explorer*, that was built by the CIA in the late 1960s and early 1970s. The *Glomar Explorer* was intended to salvage a sunken Soviet submarine and its three nuclear missiles. Though the press got wind of the project while it was ongoing, the CIA convinced the media not to publish the story for national security reasons. While the *Glomar Explorer* mission was still underway, a journalist filed a Freedom of Information request with the CIA asking for documents about the boat. The agency responded that it could neither confirm nor deny the existence of those documents. The journalist took the CIA to court, but a judge upheld the legality of the answer. The term *Glomar response* had entered the vernacular.

What's most interesting to me about the *Glomar* story is that eventually the information was declassified. Around 2010, the CIA released many of the original documents on the top-secret boat. One of the crew members of the *Glomar Explorer* even wrote a book about it. All of that neither confirming nor denying by the CIA was, in fact, hiding something. Nevertheless, the Glomar response continues to be widely deployed. It has been used to cover both far-afield conspiracy theories and well-documented, seemingly innocuous events. The CIA has neither confirmed nor denied possessing information on everything from the Brazilian president's widely publicized visit to Langley in 2019 to mind control experiments to the Kennedy assassination.

For my own purposes, the CIA's response gave me no indication about the extent of my father's covert work. But it's the white space surrounding the answers that I find the most revealing. And it wasn't the only letter that made me suspicious. The next FOIA response came from the FBI:

> We're contacting you about the FOIA request above. The FBI located approximately 4,060 pages potentially responsive to your request.
>
> Requests are processed in the order in which they are received through our multi-track processing system:
>
> Small track requests (0–50 pages) current average time is approximately 4 months to complete;
> Medium track requests (51–950 pages) current average time is approximately 29 months to complete;
> Large track requests (951–8000 pages) current average time is approximately 60 months to complete; and
> Extra-large track requests (over 8000 pages) current average time is approximately 84 months to complete.

Based on the total pages they'd found—approximately 4,060—I could expect my FOIA request to be filled in roughly sixty months, or five years. The FBI gave me the option of reducing the scope of my request down to forty-two relevant pages. This would dramatically speed up the processing time, the agency said. I agreed.

One month later, I received eleven pages. Five of those pages were photocopies of newspaper articles from the *Fort Lauderdale Sun Sentinel* about my father's case, two were memorandums stating that my father had sought citizenship in the Bahamas, one was a cover letter, and the rest were redacted beyond readability.

Along with this mailing came an official letter explaining that the remainder of the information would not be released based on several exemptions to FOIA disclosure requirements. It included its own neither-confirm-nor-deny clause:

> To the extent your request seeks records of intelligence sources, methods, or activities, the FBI can neither confirm nor deny the existence of records pursuant to FOIA exemptions (b)(1), (b)(3), and as applicable to requests for records about individuals, PA exemption (j)(2) [5 U.S.C. §§ 552/552a (b)(1), (b)(3), and (j)(2)]. The mere acknowledgment of the existence or nonexistence of such records is itself a classified fact protected by FOIA exemption (b)(1) and/or would reveal intelligence sources, methods, or activities protected by exemption (b)(3) [50 USC § 3024(i)(1)].

At the bottom of the page was a very polite send-off:

> This is the final release of information responsive to your FOIA request. This material is being provided to you at no charge.

There was one agency left on my list—the DEA. I finally heard back from them, with their own version of the Glomar response.

> Regarding your request for records on Tilton Lamar Chester, Jr., please be advised that we have decided to neither confirm nor deny the existence of such records pursuant to Exemptions 6 & 7(C) of the FOIA. *See* 5 U.S.C. § 552(b)(6), (7)(C). Even to acknowledge the existence of law enforcement records on another individual could reasonably be expected to constitute an unwarranted invasion of personal privacy.

This time, I decided to push harder. The invasion of privacy statute doesn't apply to those who are deceased. I called the helpline number listed on the letter, and the representative from the DEA's FOIA section suggested that if I could prove Tilton Lamar Chester Jr. was dead, then I would have a better chance of receiving my documents. So I sent a follow-up request with a copy of the National Transportation Safety Board report of my father's plane crash and multiple articles detailing both his death and his case. This was the agency's response:

> To retrieve the information that you may be seeking requires more specificity. Under the FOIA, an agency is not required to conduct research. DEA maintains several types of records and records systems (i.e., regulatory, personnel, investigative, etc.). For example, in your letter, you are requesting information regarding Tilton Lamar Chester, Jr., yet you have not specified a particular DEA office that you wish searched; a time frame; or the type of record that would be responsive to your request. Be advised that there are approximately 22 DEA Field Divisions, over 250 domestic offices, and more

than 150 Headquarters activities. Since your description did not limit the search to a specific office or area, a vast majority of DEA offices would be tasked to conduct a search of their respective offices for any responsive records pertaining to the subject of your request. As such, your request is overly broad and burdensome.

This is when it dawned on me that I would get nowhere with my Freedom of Information Act requests. I would run myself ragged trying to meet the demands of the FOIA system, only to continue to butt up against more exemption clauses. So, I turned in a different direction.

My uncle Tony told me to start with Iran. Then follow the money to Nicaragua. "That's where you'll find Lamar's ace in the hole."

IN 1979, THE revolution in Iran had seen the shah ousted and Ayatollah Khomeini installed in his place. Iranian students had stormed the American embassy in Tehran, believing that America was interfering in the revolution. They took fifty-two hostages. In retribution, US president Jimmy Carter imposed an arms embargo against Iran. Most of Iran's defense weapons were US-made, which meant that an arms embargo would cripple the country militarily. Still, the Iranian students would not release the hostages. The crisis dragged on over many months. A full year later, the hostages were still being held in Tehran. The arms embargo was still in place. And in the 1980 US presidential election, Ronald Reagan defeated Jimmy Carter in a landslide victory. Reagan vowed to uphold the embargo.

Meanwhile, more than eight thousand miles away, in Central

America, another revolution was underway. The left-wing Sandinistas had seized power in Nicaragua. The Sandinistas were Marxists, heavily influenced by Fidel Castro and Ché Guevara. Though the Carter administration had broached talks with the group, the staunchly anti-Communist Reagan administration refused any communication. Almost immediately after taking office in January 1981, Reagan began supporting the right-wing Contras, which vowed to remove the leftist Sandinistas.

Congress was not in favor of the idea. In fact, lawmakers were so strongly against it that they passed the Boland Amendment, which prohibited funding the Contras. If Reagan was going to continue his project, he'd need to raise money on the side. That's how his administration came to establish what was called the Enterprise, a secret organization headed by Oliver North. On Reagan's orders, the United States secretly sold arms to Iran in violation of its own 1979 embargo. The money raised from the deal was covertly funneled into arming and training the Nicaraguan Contras, Reagan's favorite anti-Communist cause.

While the arms deals were taking place in Iran, weapons dealers within the Enterprise had to find a way to ferry guns and munitions to the rebels in Nicaragua. Because the US wasn't allowed to openly support the Contras, they couldn't use the usual routes. American military planes would not be making any trips to the jungles on the Nicaraguan border. So, who would fly the guns down?

The CIA knew that smugglers were running marijuana and cocaine out of Central and South America. They knew that the smugglers were skillful bush pilots, adept at landing on difficult runways. They knew that most of the aircraft used for smuggling were already equipped with short takeoff and landing gear. And the business logic was obvious. The smugglers would fly the arms down to the Contras, and on the return trip they'd fill their empty holds with dope. In exchange, federal agents would look the other way. If the smugglers got caught, they'd have a get-out-of-jail-free card.

In other words, they'd have an ace in the hole.

AS INCONCEIVABLE AS this sounds, there's plenty of documentation to back it up. Pulitzer Prize–winning reporter Gary Webb wrote about it extensively for the *San Jose Mercury News*. Interestingly, Webb shared my frustration with the FOIA system. "Every Freedom of Information Act request I filed was rejected on national security or privacy grounds, was ignored, or was responded to with documents so heavily censored they must have been the source of much hilarity down at the FOIA offices," Webb wrote. Former smugglers testified about the guns-for-drugs system in front of a subcommittee of the Senate Foreign Relations Committee chaired by John Kerry, then a senator from Massachusetts. Two men jumped up during Oliver North's congressional testimony during the Iran-Contra scandal, holding a sign that read "Ask about the cocaine smuggling" before they were dragged from the room. (North has continually denied that the Enterprise sold drugs for arms.) And the story of Barry Seal—perhaps the most famous commercial pilot turned drug smuggler turned gunrunner—was popularized in the Tom Cruise film *American Made*.

It's no stretch to imagine that my father, who perfectly fit the profile of these other smugglers, was approached about running guns to the Contras. In fact, the year before he died, he told a friend he was planning to buy a De Havilland DHC-6–200. The De Havilland was a turboprop twin-engine utility aircraft with a reputation for reliability. Like the Cessna 206, it was known as a workhorse. The biggest difference between the 206 and the De Havilland was the carry load: the De Havilland could handle up to five thousand pounds. Why would a man who had staked his smuggling operation on small personal aircraft suddenly switch to a turboprop twin-engine that would definitely get noticed by the authorities? Because he wasn't worried about the authorities.

When my father was holding press conferences and being interviewed for the newspapers, he promised reporters a massive story. He claimed it was a story that would dismantle people's faith in the US government. Was he talking about the fact that drug smugglers were running guns to the Contras in Nicaragua with knowledge of forces in the CIA and even potentially President Reagan? Was it because this was in direct opposition to the Boland Amendment, and therefore illegal? That the entire operation was funded by illegal arms deals with Iran, a nation that had held Americans hostage for over a year and with which any sort of trade was prohibited? Yes, that's what I believe. Because at the moment my father was promising his story to the press—1984—the CIA's clandestine support of the Contras was still unknown to the general public. The first whisperings about Oliver North and the Enterprise wouldn't reach the news until June 1985, the same month my father was killed. The full details of the Iran-Contra Affair wouldn't be exposed until 1986.

The worst part is that multiple people who tried to reveal the CIA's drugs-for-guns system were either murdered or died under suspicious circumstances. In 1984 a Panamanian physician who'd fought with the Contras gave a detailed report about Contra cocaine trafficking to a Panamanian official. Soon afterward, the physician was horrifically tortured and murdered. Smuggler turned arms runner Barry Seal was gunned down in front of a

Salvation Army halfway house in 1986 after he testified about his gunrunning for the CIA. And Gary Webb, the journalist at the *San Jose Mercury News*, was discredited and forced out of the paper. He was later vindicated, but not before his death in 2004. He died from two gunshot wounds to the head. The Sacramento County coroner ruled it a suicide.

In the months leading up to my father's death, he spoke often to the reporters who covered his case, especially a young journalist named CB Hackworth. Sometimes my dad would call CB in the middle of the night when he couldn't sleep. In one of those conversations, my dad told CB, "They are not going to let me live out of this. They're going to make me run or they're going to kill me."

25

The Woodwork

MY FATHER—MY *FATHER*—MIGHT HAVE BEEN murdered. The truth of this possibility settled over me like a sickness. I'd wake up in the dark hours before dawn, my hair damp with sweat, and listen to the night noises outside my house while my lips clamped shut against the queasiness in my gut.

I needed more information, so I began to track down the people who had been in my father's circle. I started with a man named Victor Obert. Obert had been one of my father's boyhood friends and also a pilot for Eastern. After Eastern folded, Obert was hired by the National Transportation Safety Board as a crash investigator.

"Are you sure you want to do this?" Obert asked the first time I called him. "If it is what it appears to be, I'm not sure you better delve into this. For your own sake."

I sat at my writing desk, the phone in my hand, while summer rains drummed against the metal roof. "I'm sure," I told him.

In the early 2000s, Obert told me, he was called to Alabama to investigate a crash. The investigation team spent a week in the same hotel. In the evenings, after work, they'd sit at the bar and have a drink together. One evening, Obert was chatting with the man from the plane's engine manufacturer, who was also part of the crash investigation team. The man was older than Obert and had worked aviation accidents throughout the South for decades. As it turned out, he'd been part of the investigation team on my father's crash.

"There was something funny about that plane crash," he told Obert in the hotel bar. "The investigators came up with this theory that it had run out of gas, but that never did sit right with me. It always felt like they were trying to cover something up."

I BEGAN TO reach out to the family members and friends who had been exiled from my life. I was hesitant at first, uncertain if they'd even speak to me, convinced that they must be wrapped in the same secrecy that I had known most of my life. But that wasn't the case at all. In fact, it was the opposite. People were happy to hear from me and glad to talk about my dad. One person put me in touch with the next person, and before long I was speaking to my aunts and cousins and my dad's old friends, people who had passed through our house in Georgia, who'd known me as a kid. I was floored by the warmth of their responses. They all said the same thing. They hadn't contacted me all these years out of respect for my mother. We'd been through a lot, they reasoned. If she needed to cut everybody off to survive, so be it. They'd honor the path she'd chosen and let her raise me without interfering. When I was ready, they'd be there, waiting.

Soon people started coming out of the woodwork. It was as if, suddenly, everyone wanted to talk about my dad. My sister Jen sent me a manila envelope full of documents she'd been holding for years, including her own Freedom of Information Act requests. My sister's letters to the Department of Justice and the State Department were dated 1988, mailed out when she was just seventeen years old. My brave, beautiful sister. My uncle Tony sent me a copy of my father's indictment and a small, harrowing stack of photos of the crash. I heard from La Venier Mize, a talented local reporter from Cleveland who had covered my father's case, and CB Hackworth, the young journalist my father used to call in the middle of the night. I got an email from a grown-up Kevin Sealy, who sent me photos of his family's stop on Darby Island during their sailing trip when he was a boy. He still remembered my dad as the coolest man he'd ever met. My father's attorney, Jeffrey Bogart, found me online, and we met for lunch in downtown Atlanta. Everyone in the restaurant seemed to know him, and people stopped by to greet him warmly. He talked about my dad in great detail. "There's no way Lamar didn't know how much gas was in that plane," he said. "No way."

BUT I STILL wasn't convinced. Even with what Tony said and everything I'd learned about the Iran-Contra Affair, I still believed that the plane crash that killed my father was an accident. Why? Because of my mom. "It was a stupid, stupid accident," she'd always told people, her face stony. She'd seemed certain, and her conviction had colored everything about how I remembered the crash and my father.

When my mom and I finally started speaking about my dad, we didn't talk about the crash. Instead she gave me things, like her Seminole wedding dress and my father's bear-claw necklace. One night, at dinner, she handed me four silver rings set with turquoise that had belonged to my dad. "You should get these resized for your fingers," she said. Now I wear them every day. She also gave me her old photo albums. There were many pictures. Of him. Of her. Of me. Of my grandparents Art and Jewel. My father was young in most of them, and he had an easy, casual air. He was usually laughing. There was an overwhelming amount of love in these photos that had been hidden. I picked out my favorite—the Polaroid taken in my dad's Boston Whaler off the coast of Little Darby when I was four months old—and I pinned it above my writing desk. There's such gentleness in the photo, such intimacy and connection between my dad and me. It's in the way he holds me. It's how his body shifts toward mine, and my small body curves toward his. It's in the way he smiles. And there is something else, something I can only think to call *mirroring*. It's a posture, an attitude, in this baby girl that reflects the man behind her. They have the same set to their shoulders, the same unflinching way of looking at the camera.

There came a point when I couldn't avoid talking about the crash with my mom any longer. I needed to ask her directly about what people were telling me. I needed to know why, in the face of so much evidence, she still claimed the plane crash was an accident.

"Do you really think it was an accident?" I asked her. "I know that's what you always told everyone . . ."

She blinked once, twice. The toughness that defines her wavered for just a moment.

"What else could I say?" she said. "We were all alone, just you and me. We had no one to protect us." Her eyes glazed over with tears, but she was careful not to let them fall. I realized then that my mom had been scared, and it must have been fear that played a part in her silence all these years. She swallowed hard, and her voice cracked when she spoke. "I was supposed to die in the plane that day too."

Ron Elliott

AFTER RON ELLIOTT'S RELEASE FROM prison in the early 2000s, he vanished into the wind. No one knew where he was. I needed to find him soon; I sensed that time was running out. The smugglers from the 1970s and 1980s who had survived dangerous plane crashes, run-ins with the law, and stints in prison were ultimately succumbing to the same thing—age.

Late one night, in a deep internet search, I discovered half of Ron's email address. The other half was filled in with asterisks. It looked like the missing part might be the name of a small town in Florida near Lake Okeechobee. I took a guess and filled in the blanks. I sent an email off to that address, introducing myself and leaving my phone number.

Ron called me early the next morning.

"A.J., this is your uncle Ron," he said.

Ron was living on a ranch near Lake Okeechobee. He offered to come down and take me to lunch the next day.

IT'S HARD NOT to wonder at life's complicated turnings. There I was, preparing to have lunch with my father's best friend, a man who had been in prison for half my life. In a different world, Ron would have been an important part of my own story, coming and going from my life the way he did on the farm. But nothing had turned out the way it might have in that other world.

Ron Elliott pulled into my driveway at noon the next day. He drove a faded blue sedan with sheepskin covers on the seats. He wore a denim shirt with pearl snap buttons, clean and pressed, and a pair of neat blue jeans with soft leather boots. He cried when he saw me, and I cried too. He told me that he'd heard that my mom didn't want any contact with people from the old days, and that's why he hadn't searched me out.

"I could have run you down," he said, "but I thought it would be an imposition."

I thought of something a friend had told me once: *We're all just waiting to hear from each other.*

Ron and I went to lunch at a nearby café, where he ordered fried chicken and stewed okra and corn fritters. I sat and listened as he talked and talked—about raising Wagyu cattle, about living in China after he was released from prison, about astronomy.

"Last night I discovered that four and a half million years ago the day was only four hours and nineteen minutes long, and the moon was a lot closer. Can you imagine how huge it must have been? It's exciting to think about."

He talked endlessly, the subjects only loosely connected, and I wondered where it was all going. Right then, he stopped.

"I have to tell you that for the last five years I've been struggling with dementia," he said. "I struggle with it every day."

And then he slipped off into another topic.

When he finally took a breath, I jumped in.

"I heard that you might know what happened to my dad," I said.

He paused. Then he sighed. "It's going to be hard to tell you some of this."

"I know," I said, "but I need to hear it."

What he said next, he told me with perfect clarity. I listened over the rattle of plates and cutlery, surrounded by the smell of hot grease and the chitchat of waitresses and working men. Ron's day-to-day experience was complicated by the dementia that plagued his brain, but he had pockets of long-term memory that remained perfectly intact. That day in the restaurant, I asked him about what he knew in great detail. Over the months that followed, I saw him again and spoke to him many times on the phone. Each time I asked about the story he told me that day in the restaurant, and each time he retold it with unvarying precision. It never shifted or altered.

NOT LONG AFTER I saw Ron, I got a message from my dad's buddy in the years before the crash, Durbin McCollum, who'd also been a pilot for Eastern. He lived in North Georgia and had been to the farm many times. Durbin had found me online and tracked down my email address. "You were only five years old the last time I saw you," he wrote. "Please get in touch. I just recently received some information regarding you and Lamar's airplane crash. If you care to hear the 'how and why,' I finally know. Be looking forward to hearing from you. Love, Durbin."

Durbin was at his cabin in the mountains of North Carolina when I called. It was early evening, and he'd poured himself a drink. He was sitting outside on the porch, watching the fog come down off the hills. He lived by himself, he told me; "Any time a woman so much as hangs a sweater in my closet, I start to get jumpy." His son, Ethan, lived in the next town over. I blushed when he mentioned Ethan's name. I remembered being a little girl and thinking Ethan was the most handsome man in the world.

"How's your mom?" Durbin asked.

"It's hard to tell," I said.

He made an *mmm-hmm* sound. "She always was a private person."

He'd seen that I'd already published my first book, and he told me he was proud of me.

"It's hard to make your mark on the world," he said. "I guess you seen that."

"I have."

We talked some more, and eventually we reached the reason for our call. He'd recently heard a story that confirmed that my father's plane was sabotaged, he said. He wanted to share it with me. Would I come to Georgia to see him?

I said I would.

We hung up, and I bought a plane ticket to Atlanta.

Homecoming

IN ALL OF MY CONVERSATIONS with people who had known my father, we rarely talked about the farm in Georgia. There wasn't much to say. The land had been sold and part of it turned into a rock quarry. The house had been torn down, people said. That's what I believed until I spoke to La Venier Mize. La Venier had been a young reporter in White County when my father was alive. She'd written a number of articles about him and been out to the farm many times to interview him. She still lived in Cleveland.

"Are you going to visit your old house?" she asked when I told her over the phone that I was coming to Atlanta.

I shook my head. "It's been torn down."

"Torn down?" La Venier laughed. "Are you at your computer? Look up Blue Hollow Retreat in North Georgia."

I typed the words into my laptop. In seconds I was staring at a photo of the living room of the house my father built. It looked exactly like I remembered. My eyes filled with tears.

"That's my house," I said to La Venier. "It's still there."

The house was owned by a Baptist church in a nearby North Georgia town. It had been reborn as a retreat center. Some of the inside had been renovated, I could see from the photos, but the structure was essentially the same. Instantly, I knew I needed to get inside. I needed to be there, to be surrounded by its walls. I needed to walk the property, to breathe its mountain air, to stand beneath its trees. And as much as I was afraid to, I knew I needed to visit the crash site, the field where my father had died.

The website listed a number to call for reservations, and I dialed it immediately. I told the kind-sounding woman on the phone that I was looking for a place to hold a writing retreat for ten of my friends. I hated to lie, but that old shame was there again. I worried that they might turn me away if they knew who I was.

"For an overnight stay, we can sleep up to twenty-two people comfortably," the woman said. "It's set up more as a camp with mostly bunk beds. As far as a writers' retreat, you all would have plenty of room to be separate and then have lots of stuff to do—kayaking, canoeing, fishing, hiking. It's beautiful up there."

Yes, I wanted to tell her. I remember.

"We have what we call the main house," the woman from the church continued. "It has five bedrooms and a designated restroom for men and a restroom for women. There's a large main dining room usually set up with tables and chairs for forty to forty-five people. We've got a large kitchen with everything you could possibly need, a large raised patio, a front room with vaulted ceilings. There's porches all over the house and a lot of quiet places. Rocking chairs, hiking trails, tennis courts with basketball hoops. And acres and acres and acres of land that surround the retreat's main house."

My mind reeled. She was describing my childhood home to me—the tennis courts, the wooded hills, the rocking chairs. I thought about the dining room that now sat forty-five, and imagined forty-five people in the house that once was a private home for my family. I thought of everything that had made the house unique and glamorous, but it wasn't the fancy parts that I missed. It was the energy of the house, the feeling of being inside, the way it once held my happiest memories. For a brief moment, I felt a shattering loss. I thought of all the people who had passed through our house in the time since we had lost the farm. While we had lived in exile, they had gone on building fires in the fireplaces and cooking meals in the kitchen and sitting on the front porch while the lightning bugs gathered in the dusk. It wasn't the loss that mattered, I knew. What mattered was that the house was still standing, and there was a very real possibility that I could return to it.

I asked the woman on the phone about pricing.

She sounded almost apologetic. "Well, the minimum is three hundred dollars a night."

It was a price I'd be willing to pay so that I could be in the house where my best and brightest memories resided. It was a world I had believed lost, and here it was, a living space.

"I'll take July seventh," I said as calmly as I could.

"Wonderful," the woman told me. "Milton Percy is the on-site director. He gives tours, helps people with anything they need. Milton will be the one to call you and schedule your arrival. It may take him a little bit to get back to you. A lot of times he's out on the tractor. You know how it is."

Yes, I thought. I know how it is.

SEEING THE PHOTOS of the house on the retreat's website filled me with an intense longing. I deeply missed our beautiful home with its wood paneling and peaked wood ceilings, its stone fireplaces and wraparound porch. But I was worried too. What if I got there, only to be disappointed? What if I discovered that the house I had imagined as an idyll could not live up to my memories? What if I left worse off than I'd gone? Perhaps I was diving too deep into a story I could never get my hands around. Maybe my mother's instincts had been right, and the only way forward was to leave this all behind.

I flew to Atlanta plagued by these doubts, outrunning a hurricane that was set to hit the Gulf Coast of Florida. It was raining in Georgia when I landed, a light summer rain with none of the ferocity of the storm I'd left behind. My GPS told me the drive to Cleveland would take an hour and a half. The traffic made me nervous with its fast-moving cars, many lanes, and quick exits. My stomach roiled. Atlanta was unfamiliar to me, yet there was a moment, on a curve on the outskirts of the city, a short stretch of the highway that was momentarily empty and bordered by tall pines, when recognition swelled in my body. But then the traffic caught me and the curve passed and I was back in the concrete raceways of I-85.

It took me a while to get out of the city, and a longer while to get out of the suburban sprawl that surrounds it, but eventually I found myself on a stretch of rural road going north. I stopped at a gas station to use the bathroom. A sign on the beer cooler inside read "No beer sales before 8 a.m." Back outside, the air was cool, the sky clouded. It was July 7, 2021. Thirty-six years and seventeen days since the plane crash. I took a long, steadying breath and got in the car.

I hadn't told anyone I was in Georgia. Not my friends, not my sister, not my mother. I wanted to make the trip alone. My phone pinged with people asking how I was faring in the hurricane. *I'm surviving*, I said. I thought about sitting in the gas station parking lot a little longer, but my GPS scolded me. *Head north. Head north. Head north.*

A little farther up the road, I drove past a roadside stand that sold hot boiled peanuts. I considered buying a bag and sitting in my car, splitting the shells with my teeth. Instead, I pressed forward, anxious to arrive and also afraid. The afraid part telling me to stop. The anxious part saying, *Go*. Breathe, I told myself. Breathe.

I drove along a narrow two-lane highway that ran between tall trees thick with summer leaves. Corn grew in flat parcels beside the road. Signs for fresh peaches were stuck in the ground. Everything was unfamiliar and yet, deeper down, achingly familiar.

The GPS told me to turn right onto a stretch of unpaved road, and when I did, gravel crunched under the tires in a way that I knew. *I knew*. Straight ahead, a road went up the mountain. To my left sat an old house in terrible shape, nearly falling down. I realized, sadly, that it was the guesthouse where my grandparents Art and Jewel had always stayed. And if that was the guesthouse, then that meant, farther away, on the road that led to the left, was the field where the plane had gone down. But I wasn't ready for that yet. First I wanted to see the place where my dad had lived, not where he had died.

I turned right onto a long dirt road bordered by empty pastures. There were trees lining the road but no cattle in the fields. I drove slowly until I saw the house. It looked exactly the way it had thirty years ago. Hot tears sprang to my eyes. Not from sadness, but from relief. And joy. And gratitude.

The retreat's director, Milton Percy, stood on the deck. He was dressed in a dark cotton T-shirt and a pair of khaki shorts. He wore heavy-duty hiking boots and tall dark socks. His face was tanned from the sun. He looked like a man who spent most of his time outdoors and was glad of it.

I parked my rental car in the driveway. When I opened the car door, two cats came to brush against my legs. I knelt down and scratched their backs while Milton asked politely about the traffic in Atlanta.

I stepped onto the deck, and we shook hands. Milton radiated warmth and good humor. His eyes were kind, and I felt instantly at ease.

"Do you want the two-minute tour or the fifteen-minute tour?" he asked.

"I'll take the fifteen-minute tour," I said, curious what a church might have to say about the property.

Milton strode through the sliding glass door, and I followed him inside, still playing the role of stranger to this place. But once I crossed the threshold, a wave of nostalgia hit me. It was so strong that I almost stumbled. I could feel my eyes wanting to well up. I took slow sips of air through my nose. *Deep breath*, I repeated to myself. *Deep breath.*

What had struck me was the smell. The wood paneling and the hardwood floors were both original to the house. They gave off a woodsy smell that reminded me of home. Because I *was* home. I felt it deep in my stomach, and that's when I knew I had not made a mistake in coming.

"I've been here six years," Milton was saying. He stood in the doorway from the front room to the renovated dining area. "In the first six months I was here, I heard seventy versions of this story."

What story? I thought. Surely a Baptist retreat center wasn't going to talk about my drug smuggling father. But then Milton said, "The house was built by a guy named Lamar Chester."

My breath caught in my throat.

"Lamar had been an Eastern Airlines pilot in the 1960s and '70s. You may or may not know, but in the '70s and '80s, drug smuggling was a big business, and Lamar Chester became a drug smuggler. That hay field out there is where he used to land his planes . . ."

I sat on the spare utilitarian couch in the front room of my father's house, listening to a stranger tell me my dad's story. It was the version that had been in the papers, nothing I didn't already know, but still it was uncanny.

"Lamar and his wife lived here without making any waves, but then in 1983 he came under federal indictment," Milton told me.

I followed along, nodding, though of course I knew where the story was headed. My father was indicted in '83, he said he was a covert agent in '84, his trial was scheduled for the summer of '85, but then the crash—

Milton was still talking, but my belly had tied itself into a painful knot.

"In 1985, before he could go to trial, Lamar's plane crashed in a field on the property," Milton said. "Sadly, his little girl was in the plane with him."

Until this moment, I'd managed to keep myself together. I hadn't revealed just how unbalanced I felt. But at the mention of the crash, I couldn't hold it in any longer. I put my hands over my face and started to cry. Milton, concerned, asked if I was all right.

"I'm sorry," I said.

Milton looked stricken. "Did I say something?"

"No. It's not your fault. I didn't want to say anything, but you started telling that story . . ."

Milton looked at me with his mouth open, his face awash with understanding. "It's you, isn't it?" he said. "The little girl."

I took my hands away from my face. "I was afraid if I told the church who I was, they wouldn't let me stay in the house."

Milton's voice was gentle. "I saw your name on the booking—Artis—and I knew that was your mom's name. I thought it might be you."

"It's me," I said.

"What are you doing here?"

"I'm trying to learn about my dad," I told him, worried he might be angry that I was prying into a story that was better forgotten. Instead, he lit up.

"I've got so many people you need to meet," he said excitedly.

It took me a second to understand. "People remember my dad?"

"Anyone who was alive in 1980 remembers Lamar Chester."

Milton started naming off the people I should speak to: the farmer who owned the plot of land just south of the property, the farmer who owned the land to the east, the neighbors up the mountain, the doctor who lived on the very top of the mountain. The good thing about a place like Cleveland, Georgia, he told me, is that it's a small town. Even better, people rarely leave.

"But all these people," I said, "they'd talk to me?"

I thought about how my dad was a shameful secret in my own family, how no one spoke about him. Now everyone in North Georgia, it seemed, was willing to share what they knew.

"Of course," Milton said. "Half the county believes your dad is still alive and in witness protection."

Talking fast, nearly dancing from foot to foot, Milton relayed the stories he'd heard. A bug exterminator once peeked into a closet he was never allowed to spray, and the closet was packed with stacks of hundred-dollar bills. Some people said my father had turned his cash into krugerrands, gold coins from South Africa. People were sure he'd hidden the gold somewhere on the property, and they'd been all over the mountain with metal detectors looking for it. I sat there with my mouth open. All this time, when I had kept silent, willfully erasing my dad's memory, he'd lived on as a legend in White County, Georgia.

Then Milton told me another story that many locals believe, but it was hard for me to hear.

"When the crash happened," he said, "the story is that you crawled out and ran to the highway to flag someone down to help your daddy."

It's a good story. In some ways, I wish it were true. If it were, then that would mean my injuries weren't as severe as they actually were, and that I had been a hero. I shook my head. "My grandpa pulled me out of the plane."

Then I asked him how the house came to be a retreat center. "I heard it had been torn down and turned into a gravel mine."

"Shortly after you left, a guy bought the five hundred acres for the mineral rights," he said. He pointed toward the road I'd driven in on and the now-dilapidated guesthouse. "You can see on that side of the property where there's a rock quarry. Since the 1980s, they've taken down a large part of the mountain."

Our beautiful mountain, I thought.

After the five hundred acres were sold, the new owner kept half for the granite mine, and in the mid-1990s he sold the other half. The new owners had a chain of local grocery stores. They used the house and the land as a family getaway on weekends and holidays over the next decade. When the patriarch passed away, his wife donated the house and 170 acres to the church. That's how it became the retreat center.

As I was trying to process everything he'd just said, Milton reached for his phone. "I'll start making calls," he said and headed outside. As the door closed behind him, I heard him saying, "It's her."

While he was on the phone, I went out through the back door. I expected to see the pool where my dad and I had spent afternoons swimming, but the pool had been filled in. This hit me hard, harder than the other renovations. It was the first time I understood that this was no longer the home I'd grown up in.

I walked to where the pool had once been, now a tract of seamless grass, and I knelt down and ran my hands over the earth, remembering all the people I had known in this house—not just my father but the friends and relatives, the exuberant carnival passing by. The writer Thomas Wolfe famously said that we can never go home again, and as I knelt in the grass, I knew the truth of it.

I stood and dusted off my hands. I circled the house and started to walk toward the tall trees that once hid my secret spot, the clear creek that ran over smooth stones.

"Where you headed?" Milton called out from the porch.

"There used to be a creek over here," I said, pointing.

He shook his head. "The creek dried up years ago."

When I got back to the front porch, Milton was leaning against the railing and going through his phone.

"I'm thinking of who else to call," he said.

The two cats I'd met earlier appeared from beneath my car. They came to rub against my legs.

"You won't believe what we named them," Milton said.

I squatted down to pet one of them. "What?"

"Lamar and Chester."

I shook my head, laughing quietly. "When did the renovations happen?" I asked.

"That sunken Jacuzzi was still there up until five years ago," Milton told me. "I'd take people and show them around, and when we got to the big tub, you could imagine Al Pacino in there, like in *Scarface*."

I thought of my father, always gentle with me, sitting with one of our cats in his lap or swimming in the pool or working the farm on his tractor. And I thought of Tony Montana from *Scarface*, face down in a mound of cocaine, brandishing his machine gun. Were they even close to being the same man? Maybe, to someone from the outside, they were.

In order to make the house into a church retreat, Milton said, the Jacuzzi had to go. So did the bar. He shook his head. "We can't have a Baptist retreat with a bar."

He told me the church's renovations had also covered up the stairwell that led down to the crawlspace. "We thought for sure if there's gold, it's there," Milton said. "But we already looked."

SOON EVERYONE STARTED to arrive, some Milton had called and some I had called. Friends of my father, neighbors, residents of Cleveland. We sat on the front porch, rocking softly and talking. It was wonderful to see everyone after years of isolating myself, but what I couldn't stop thinking about was the last wound I had ever wanted to reopen, the story of the plane crash. Some of these people had been there. Would they have the answer to the questions that had haunted me my whole life?

Perhaps Dr. Mike Eberhardt might. Dr. Eberhardt, a family physician, had lived at the top of the mountain since the 1980s. He came to the house and sat inside in one of the spare chairs that now furnished the front room. He started by asking me what I remembered about the crash. It's an old question by now, a familiar question. I told him the truth: not much. He nodded.

"It may not be available to you because it was wiped out by a concussion," he said. "You had your bell rung pretty good, good enough for there to be no memories."

My body seemed to release something in that moment, an old tension I didn't realize I'd been holding. The fact that I have few memories, both just before the crash and after, might have a physiological explanation. Maybe I hadn't failed my father by forgetting those moments. I simply didn't have a choice.

"Tell me about the day of the crash," I said to Dr. Eberhardt.

"That day I was coming home from work in the evening," he said. "It was around five thirty. The office closes at five, but I've got all this other bullshit I've got to do. Clean up, that sort of thing.

"The ambulance passed me on the road, and I saw that they were turning in the driveway. I just followed them in." Dr. Eberhardt shook his head. "Lamar was two hundred yards from his own airstrip. He almost made it." I felt the weight of that land in my solar plexus, as painful as a physical blow.

When Dr. Eberhardt arrived at the crash site, the local sheriff's officers and the EMS workers were just standing around the crash site. "Twiddling their thumbs," he said. I'd already been taken away in an ambulance. My mom had gone with me. My grandparents followed in their car. That left the crash site to the officers, EMS workers, and my father's body. Dr. Eberhardt asked them why they hadn't taken my dad out of the plane.

"The Georgia Bureau of Investigation agent pronounced him dead but told us not to touch him," one of the men standing around the plane said.

"I'm pretty sure that GBI man is not a doctor," Dr. Eberhardt said. "I'm the only doctor here, and I'm the only one who can pronounce him dead. Give me the hook knife."

One of the men handed Dr. Eberhardt the knife, and he slit the seat belt straps that held my father in place. He had a brief, terrible moment of realization—his friend was dead, and he was holding his body—before his clinical impulses took over. They maneuvered my dad out of the plane and stretched him on the wing. His blood smeared across the metal. One of his shoes slipped off. Dr. Eberhardt inspected the body.

"At that point it was obvious from feeling his head that his neck was broken," he told me. "He was damaged beyond doing anything."

Dr. Eberhardt must have seen the way the color left my face, or how very still I sat when he told me this information, because he took a deep breath and turned in a different direction.

"Lamar was not a careless man," he said. "He was a careful pilot. He would have been doubly careful with you." Dr. Eberhardt said he couldn't imagine a circumstance in which my father wouldn't refuel the plane after his last flight and then, in his preflight checklist, wouldn't notice that the plane had low fuel. It just wasn't the kind of pilot he was.

I nodded, though my journalist's brain leaned hard against the seams of this. But what about the crash in the Everglades, with Pop and Vera, when my father *had* run out of gas? He had pushed his plane to the outer limits on that flight, and his calculated risk had failed. But Dr. Eberhardt said my father was not a careless man. And I knew that the crash in the Everglades had served to reinforce his caution. Going forward, he never made that mistake again.

What Dr. Eberhardt was saying echoed what my uncle Tony had said. The plane had not, in fact, run out of gas, at least not because of any miscalculation on my father's part. Dr. Eberhardt and my uncle Tony would not have crossed paths after my father died. Tony was already in witness protection by then, far away from Georgia. The two men hadn't known each other when he was alive. Yet, separately and independently, they'd come to the same conclusion about his death.

AFTER DR. EBERHARDT left, I had a brief moment to myself. I sat outside in the cool mountain air. The afternoon was quickly moving toward evening. It had been wonderful to see everyone, and being in the house was one of the most sweetly surreal experiences of my life. But it had been hard, too. Even with all the love I felt, I'd had to turn my attention to the wound I'd spent most of my life avoiding, the one thing everyone insisted on talking about—the crash that had killed my father. I was emotionally wrung out and heart-sore in the aftermath, but there was still more to uncover.

The sun had set and a pink dusk was suffusing the sky when a car came rolling up the driveway. It was Durbin McCollum, my father's friend from Eastern, the reason I had flown to Georgia on this trip in the first place. His son, Ethan, was with him. Durbin was neat and put-together in khaki shorts, a black polo shirt, and loafers, a pair of reading glasses tucked into his collar. He looked more like a retired accountant than someone who had spent a portion of his life on the wrong side of the law.

"It's strange to think the last time I saw you, you were a little girl," Durbin said when he got out of the car and hugged me. "But I guess it must be strange for you, too. I wasn't an old man the last time you saw me."

It *was* strange. I was trying to fit a lifetime's worth of people and stories into a few short hours. My nerves were on fire. I'd hummed with a ferocious brightness all day, but now it was evening and my own light had dimmed after burning bright for so long.

"You look overwhelmed," Durbin said to me.

I was overwhelmed but also filled with gratitude. I was grateful to the friends and neighbors who'd come, to Milton Percy, who'd generously put me in touch with them, to the church that had kept this house intact.

Durbin, Ethan, and I took seats in the rocking chairs on the front porch.

"You sure were a happy little kid," Durbin said. "You were always yanking your clothes off. Around the farm, you'd be running around in the nude. That was A.J. Everybody would laugh about it."

I smiled, remembering. Durbin talked a little more about what the farm had been like when my father was alive, and he and Ethan compared memories for a bit. This was a homecoming for all of us. Like me, they hadn't sat on this porch in thirty years. We enjoyed that shared sweetness for a while, each of us remembering another time when the world felt like a safer place. But we couldn't stay there forever.

Durbin sighed and looked out over the twilight-shadowed mountains.

"The whole thing stinks," he said.

I nodded. "I know."

"The plane didn't run out of gas. You can take that one to the bank."

Ethan sat forward in his chair. Like Durbin and my father, he was also a pilot.

"A.J., there's no way your dad would have gotten in that plane with no fuel in it. There's no way. When a pilot gets in an airplane, he checks his fuel gauge. That's one of the first things he's going to do. He's going to check his gauge and then he's going to check the fuel visually."

"Every time?" I asked.

"Every single time," Ethan said. "I watched Lamar do it on all his planes. It wasn't something he took lightly."

"Another thing," Durbin said. "There's no way, even if he did lose that engine, that he would have rolled that plane upside down. Even a student pilot wouldn't do that. He was probably the most experienced light airplane pilot that I've ever seen."

Ethan agreed. "That was such a nontypical crash for that type of airplane. I've never heard of anybody doing that. Ever. He was amazing with any kind of single-engine plane. He's not going to wind up upside down."

The evening had edged toward dark. The three of us sat quietly, contemplating what this meant. I'd spent most of my life believing the crash was an accident, and it took an overwhelming amount of evidence to convince me it wasn't. We were nearly at that point.

"Do you have any photos of the crash?" Ethan asked me.

I pulled out the stack of pictures my uncle Tony had given me. They passed the photos back and forth between them.

"You see this right here?" Durbin said, pointing to one of the wing struts. "The only way it would look like that is if a bolt was missing."

"Of course we don't know, because the plane never came back from the National Transportation Safety Board after the crash," Ethan said.

Durbin nodded. "It just disappeared."

I shivered despite the warmth of the evening. The frogs around the pond sent up a high chirping. I was afraid to ask for more, but I had to know.

"You said in your email that you knew the how and why behind the crash," I said to Durbin.

He stared thoughtfully across the mountains. Then he seemed to sink down into himself. He started off on what sounded like a tangent, about a friend of his, Leonard, who ran an upholstery shop in North Georgia. Most of Leonard's work was on private airplanes, though he also outfitted the interiors of RVs and motor homes. One day, a man named Redmond Wells came into his shop. Redmond needed some work done on his motor home. Reupholstering is a slow business, and it takes time. Redmond and Leonard got to be friendly, and eventually Leonard admitted that he used to run marijuana in California in the heyday of smuggling. Then Redmond, also being friendly, admitted he used to work for the DEA. At one point, Leonard told Redmond a weird story about something that had happened to him back in 1987.

Leonard kept his plane, a Piper J-3 Cub, in a hangar at the Cartersville airport. Durbin McCollum—who was a big-time smuggler high on the DEA's target list—also kept his plane there, a similar J-3 with the same paint job. The two planes were tied down side by side. Leonard was looking to sell his plane, and one day a guy came in wanting to see it. Leonard was out for the day, so the secretary let the guy in. He spent a lot of time with the plane by himself. The weird part was that the guy came back the next day, when Leonard was there. He pointed to a missing bolt on the wing and told Leonard, "You're missing a bolt there. If that's the way you take care of your planes, I don't want anything to do with it." Leonard went over and looked at the wing with the missing bolt. "I'll be damned," he said. A bolt like that doesn't just slip off. It needs to be taken off by hand. After the man left, Leonard couldn't stop thinking about how the stranger had been alone with both his aircraft and Durbin's. He told Durbin the story, and the two men decided the man had been sent to rig Durbin's plane. But he'd made a mistake and taken the bolt off the wrong plane. It was only when the agent got back to the office that he ran the tail number and realized his mistake. That's why he'd come back the next day to point out the missing bolt.

The upholstery shop was empty when Leonard told this story. Still, Redmond Wells had glanced around as if to make sure. Then he'd leaned across the counter, his voice low but not so low that he could hide the fact that he was bragging. "That's how we got his buddy, Lamar Chester."

ON THE PORCH, I sat very still. All the pieces were finally fitting together.

"Do you remember Ron Elliott?" I asked quietly. Both Durbin and Ethan nodded. "He told me a story about the night before my dad died."

The day before the crash, Ron Elliott told me when we met, he'd flown to the farm for a visit. He'd had drinks with my dad and played foosball with me. My mom cooked dinner, and afterward my dad and Ron spent the evening on the concrete deck above the hangar. They drank rum and Cokes and talked about my dad's upcoming trial.

Around 10:30 p.m., Ron turned in. He was staying in the bedroom on the side of the house that sat above the hangar. The bedroom windows were open. The farm was quiet at night, no talking neighbors, no rattling truck engines from the road. The occasional hoot of an owl traveled through the hills, but otherwise the night was still.

In the bedroom above the hangar just after midnight, Ron was still awake, reading. A light rain fell outside. He listened to the patter through the open window and wondered if he would be able to take off in the morning. The house was silent around him. That's when Ron heard motors running in the driveway. He folded the corner of the page that he was on and set his book on the nightstand. He switched off the light beside the bed so that he wouldn't be backlit and then he eased out of bed and opened the bedroom door. He crept down the hallway to the front of the house and slid open the sliding glass door. Noises were coming from the hangar.

"Hey, boy, is that you?" he called, thinking it might be my father.

But my father was coming down the hallway in his underwear.

"Somebody's in the hangar," Ron said.

The quick sound of dropped metal tools and running feet came from below.

"Go get the truck," my dad said to Ron. "I'll get the shotgun."

The two men raced to the garage and jumped in the truck. They saw the taillights of two cars headed toward the main road. They chased after them, but the cars had too much of a lead. Lamar and Ron watched the taillights reach the highway and disappear over the next hill.

They came back to the house, turned all the lights on in the hangar, and looked at my dad's two work planes, the Cessna 206 and the Cessna 207. Everything was in order. They didn't think to look at the Piper Cub, the little J5-A, which was just for fun and had nothing to do with the drug trade. Whoever had been in the hangar surely wouldn't be interested in it.

IT WAS LATE when I finished telling Ron's story. A few scattered lightning bugs lit up the dark in brief flashes. Durbin sat staring into the night. For a while I thought he wouldn't say anything, but when he finally spoke, his voice was rough with grief and fury.

"Lamar was going to beat them, you know," he said. "But these people, they do not lose."

28

The Field

THE NEXT MORNING DAWNED STILL and cool. *Soft* was the word that came to mind. Gentle puffs of clouds drifted across a pearl-gray sky. I had an hour before Milton would arrive, an hour to sit on the porch in a rocking chair, taking in the mountain air. The pond in front of the house was new and the magnolia tree beside the driveway had grown huge over the years, but otherwise the view was the same as when I was a kid. A cow lowed in a nearby field. One of the cats jumped in my lap and made biscuits against my belly, and I started crying. I had grown up keeping my dad a secret, afraid to mention him out loud, but his legend still lived in this house and on this mountain. In White County, Georgia, Lamar Chester was talked about with affection and a kind of sly reverence. For more than thirty years I'd hungered for a place, a history, and a people that were mine. I wanted to be seen openly, for my entire story, a story that included my dad. I didn't want to have to pretend that he wasn't who he was. Or that I'm not who I am. To be around people who had known my father, who had been with us in this house, who had seen the child I was, felt like an enormous gift.

When Milton arrived, I followed him down the side of the hill into the hangar beneath the house. It smelled like diesel and dust and engine grease. I could feel my dad there.

Milton waved me over to the edge of the concrete. "Come take a look."

Something had been written in the concrete. It was hard to read. I squinted and tilted my head sideways. Then I saw it. A date. *10/7/77.* The day my parents had moved into the house. Beneath it was an inscription in my dad's handwriting.

It was worth it!!

I'd once wondered what it felt like for my father to hold the deed to My Goal Farm in his hand. Here was my answer. In October 1977, he believed it was worth it. And if he had known what was to come? Most of the smugglers I know have no regrets. Despite prison and fines, they still look on the smuggling days as the best days in their lives.

But my father paid a heavier price than most. We all did, for the choices he made.

MILTON AND I were still in the hangar when Paul Seaboldt arrived. Paul had lived on the farm next door all his life. He'd been a teenager when my dad died, and, I learned from Milton, he'd seen our plane just before the crash.

"You look just like your mother, young lady," Paul said when he saw me.

"Everybody keeps saying that."

It had felt strange at first to come on this trip without my mom, knowing she still wasn't ready to dredge up the past, to face these people who had been a part of my parents' lives during their happier days. But the truth was, she'd had her time with my dad. I needed to find mine.

"Look, I'm straightforward," Paul was saying. "I'm going to just tell you like it was."

"That's good," I said.

"Everybody knowed Lamar was a drug smuggler. He was somewhat open with it. Nobody ever seen any drugs, but, I mean, if you come in down through yonder, he didn't put up with no bullshit. He'd meet you right out there. And he was a big man. He could carry his own weight. You could tell he wanted his privacy. I guess if he worked for the CIA and was into that, that's just natural."

It was amazing to me how easily my father's story about working as a covert agent fell off of everyone's tongue out here.

"One of the last things I remember—I can remember distinctly—is that I was on the field over there. I was on a four-wheeler getting barrels of hay rounded up. I come out of the field, and I can remember just as plain as day—I told people this many a time now—the plane was just like sitting up sideways in the air. I'm telling you, he had it just like sideways. You could see the whole bottom. I said to myself, 'Man, Lamar, you got that thing cocked up there.' If I'd a watched it fifteen more seconds, I'd have seen y'all go down."

Fifteen more seconds, and maybe we'd have the answer.

"If you got just a minute before you leave," Paul said, "I can take you up to where the plane crashed and show you within two hundred feet."

"OK."

My voice was tight. Maybe I wasn't ready.

Maybe I would never be ready.

Milton and I followed Paul's truck in my rental car all the way to a field at the far edge of the property. Paul stopped his truck and got out.

"You're sure this is it?" I asked.

"I'm positive," he said. "Right there. A hundred percent."

He turned and headed back toward his truck, listing off the day's work he had to do between his fields and his chicken houses. "I got to get," he called over his shoulder.

Milton walked back to the car, and I stood on the edge of the field. It was bordered by tall trees. Those trees were there thirty years ago. They're in the background of all the photos of the crash. I looked out at the field, now grown over with ironweed and wildflowers. It was no more than a couple acres. I imagined it planted with rows of sweet potatoes, like it was on the day of the crash. I imagined its edges staked with grape trellises, like it was in the summer of 1985. What I couldn't imagine—though I tried—was my father landing there. It wasn't just a desperate place to land. It was an impossible place. Seeing it with my own eyes, it was finally clear—my father hadn't been trying to land there. It was simply where we fell.

I began to shake. The tall weeds waved in the morning breeze. Grasshoppers sent up a symphonic humming over the green field. I wrapped my arms around my shoulders, holding myself. On the edge of that field on a warm summer day with the grasshoppers singing in the tall grass, for the first time I truly accepted the idea that the crash—*the accident*—had never been an accident at all.

I squeezed my eyes shut, staggering under the weight of it. Heat flushed my chest and I felt a lifetime's worth of rage pass through my body, like a terrible fire scorching the earth. The first wave was anger at my father, at his insatiability, the fact that he didn't quit when he could have. Not even to protect my mom and me. And on the heels of that first wave came a second. This time, it was rage at the people who had used and discarded my dad, who had decided that he was disposable and less-than, that for all his wealth he was just a poor country kid they could throw away when they were done. I wanted to burn the whole world down, to engulf the people and places that had destroyed my father. That had, in many ways, destroyed me.

But my rage, for all its heat, couldn't burn forever. Eventually the soft breeze dried the sweat along my brow. I took a deep breath. I was wrung out and emptied, like the morning after a fever has broken.

I still had one more call to make.

29

Redmond Wells

REDMOND WELLS WAS EASY TO find online. He has a profile on LinkedIn and a phone number publicly available on the internet. Though I'd told Durbin McCollum that I wouldn't call Wells, I knew the instant I heard his name that I wouldn't stop without talking to him myself. Not because I expected him to admit the truth, but because there was something deeper at play, something more primal, more esoteric. I needed him to hear my voice.

I called the number I'd found for Wells and left a message. I said I was a writer in Florida working on a book about drug smuggling in the 1980s. I didn't say Lamar Chester was my father, though I wanted to.

I never thought Redmond Wells would call me back, but he did. Twice. I missed his first call, and when I didn't return his message within the hour, he called again.

"I remember the name Lamar Chester," he said after I answered, "but I ended up going on Google to see what happened. He had a plane, and the plane crashed with his little girl in it. I wasn't the case agent on his case. Maybe try the GBI. They worked that case, too."

His voice was cordial.

"All those old cases, they put them into the archives, but how long they keep them—or if they destroy them—I don't know," he said. "At that time, it was Customs, DEA, and GBI. We worked more smuggling cases by aircraft in Atlanta than they did in Miami. I'm not trying to brag."

That word, *brag*. It's the same word Durbin had used. He'd said Redmond Wells was bragging about what the DEA had done to my dad.

"Sorry I can't help you any more," Wells said.

He paused, as if to see if I had anything else to say. For a moment, I thought about telling him who I was. The words sat on my tongue, sharp as oyster shells, but I didn't say them. I refused to give him the chance to deny anything.

"Thank you for your time," I said, and hung up.

He would not have the final word in my story.

30

Family

MANY YEARS AGO, AT THE funeral for my father's first wife, Nancy, I remember watching my brother Terry out of the corners of my eyes. I was close to my sister Jen and my brother Bill, but Terry was a mystery to me. Like many people, he'd been exiled from my life. Yet in that moment, what I couldn't escape was the feeling of familiarity. It was as if I knew Terry, as if I'd always known him. The way he spoke, the way he moved, his sense of humor. Perhaps it was because he reflected something of our father, or maybe I remembered him from those long-ago days on the farm. Looking at him, I'd felt a sense of recognition and also affection, an instinctual part of me glad to see my brother. But there was too much separating us—too much time, too much distance, too much secrecy around our dad—for me to manage more than a brief hello.

Yet as I came to learn more about my father's story, I realized that I could not understand the complexity of it without talking to Terry. In the end, my brother Bill gave me his number and insisted I call.

THE FIRST THING Terry said to me when he picked up the phone was "What took you so long?"

Just like my visit to my uncle Tony, my phone call with Terry surprised me. Terry was smart and funny. He was a good storyteller. He talked openly about our dad and in great detail about the smuggling business. Terry lives in South Carolina with Leigh—they've been married more than forty years—and in addition to their home near the coast, they own acreage in the country where they raise cattle. He's mostly retired now, though he spent most of his career as a home builder.

Terry and I began speaking regularly in the evenings after he'd finished the day's chores and poured himself a glass of wine. We'd talk about the weather or his hopes for a spring calving before we'd settle in to the stories about our dad.

"OK, where'd we leave off?" he'd begin.

One night, deep into one of our calls, Terry said, "Let's have a sibling reunion."

"The four of us?" I asked. "In the same place?"

"I'll host it," he offered.

That's how I found myself in a car with my sister and three of her kids, heading to Terry's house in South Carolina. It was a long drive from my sister's place on Florida's east coast, and it gave me plenty of time to worry. I wore one of my dad's silver rings, and I turned it around and around on my finger. What if Terry and I didn't hit it off in person? What about his wife, Leigh, whom I knew almost nothing about, except that she had reservations about our father? I wished, briefly, that my mom could be there with all of us. But she'd made a clean break from the past. This was my moment to reconcile with it.

TERRY AND LEIGH'S house was uncannily like my house in Florida. Theirs was much grander, but the aesthetic was similar. Their house, like mine, was built in the 1920s. Mine is sided in white wood paneling, theirs is whitewashed brick. A tall oak grows in their front yard and towers over the property, shading the house with its branches. My house also has a beautiful old oak. We all saw the value in holding on to trees, I thought.

Terry and Leigh were waiting for us on the bricked front stoop. Jen and her kids got out and hugged them, but I hung back, my struggle to connect asserting itself. I looked up at the beautiful trees and down at the vines growing in the spaces between the bricks. A large feather had landed in the greenery covering the ground, and I reached down to pick it up.

"That's a barred owl feather," Terry said, walking toward me.

I was overcome with a powerful shyness. I'm an adult now, a widow, a homeowner, a published author, and yet all I could think about was hiding behind my mother's legs at the farm in Georgia and peeking out to stare up at my handsome brother. This Terry was older, but he had the same fair hair, the same blue eyes, the same jaunty way of holding his body. The barred owl feather in my hand felt special, like something the two of us now shared. I tucked it away in my bag as I followed him inside.

The interior of their house had wooden floors like mine and a curated blend of antiques and modern furnishing, also like mine. Everything had been done with an eye for style but also comfort. The plants inside the house, in particular, stood out to me. What I've come to learn about growing houseplants successfully is that they need close study. It's not that plants are particularly complicated, but to do well, they require someone who's paying attention.

"Are these your plants?" I asked Terry as he showed me around the house.

"Leigh's in charge of the plants," he said.

She's the one with the careful gaze, I thought. I remembered something Terry had said in one of our conversations, how Leigh was the only person not swept up by our dad's charms. I wondered if she saw, more clearly than most, the mix of good and bad in our father.

I followed Terry into the kitchen for a glass of water, and in a moment that was as touching as it was surprising, he leaned over and kissed me on the cheek.

"Glad you're here," he said.

I stammered, lost for words.

"Thank you for having all of us," I managed.

He grinned in a way I've come to recognize, a grin I now know was our father's. His voice was teasing but also sweet. "Well, you did this."

THE KIDS TOOK turns on the rope swing outside while the adults napped and showered, and I found myself upstairs looking through a box that Leigh had pulled from the attic for me. It was filled with old newspapers and court transcripts. I picked up the article sitting on top and read the headline: "Accused Drug Smuggler Dies in Airplane Crash Near Home." My heart hurt reading it. The more I had learned about my father, the more I grieved his loss. Yet what I had gained in exchange was worth every moment of grief. I set the article back in the box and started to turn away, but someone was coming up the stairs. It was Leigh. She had been quiet most of the day, and I had been wondering what she thought of our rowdy group descending on her neat and orderly house.

"Thank you for letting me see all this," I said. "You don't mind if I take it home with me?"

"Go ahead," Leigh said. "I hope you can use it."

There we were, alone, two women staring over a box filled with stories of my father. Leigh knew so much of our family; she'd known my dad, she'd watched Terry get involved in the business, seen the desperate way he wanted to earn our father's respect, and in the end had waited for him while he served his time. Knowing her skepticism about my father, I waited to hear what she might say, staked in place by anxiety, prepared to be wounded by some new devastating revelation about my dad's flaws, his role as a bad guy in the grand scheme of things.

Instead, she gave me something precious.

"He loved you, you know."

Hot tears sprang to my eyes, and I scrubbed at my face with the back of my hand.

"He was proud of you," she went on.

"But I was little."

Leigh shook her head. "He saw something in you. He always said he had big plans for you."

During my phone calls with Terry, Leigh had always been in the background. Sometimes he'd pause to ask her a question, or she'd correct a date he'd given me. She must have heard what I'd been asking all along, the question beneath my inquiries about Operation Lone Star and the Darby Islands and how long it took to fly a load of marijuana from Jamaica to Miami. She'd recognized my real question, the beating heart at the center of my search.

IT WAS NEARLY dusk when I made my way to a back corner of the brick terrace outside. A big wolf-dog named Sasha was stretched out on the bricks. I sat in a wrought iron chair and tilted my head back to look at the towering trees overhead. An owl called from somewhere close. I wondered if it was the same owl who'd dropped the feather I found earlier.

It wasn't long before Terry and Jen joined me. I listened as they talked about memories they shared, memories of growing up in Miami, memories of their mother. They swapped her favorite puns.

After a while, Terry asked me, "Do you tell people you have siblings?"

I wasn't sure how to answer that question. "I'll refer to my brother and sister in conversation," I told him. "So, yeah, I guess I do."

"But if someone asks if you're an only child?" he pressed.

"If someone asks like that, then yes, I tell them I'm an only child."

"Only child," Jen said, ribbing me. "Totally spoiled."

"The little princess," Terry said.

"I don't think I was spoiled," I said, bristling.

Terry and Jen cut their eyes at each other.

"Do you think Bill's little boy is spoiled?" Terry asked.

Like my dad, Bill has a second marriage and a late-in-life baby.

"Well, yeah," I admitted.

All three of us laughed.

Terry nodded. "There you have it."

What I didn't say, though it came instantly to mind and took everything I had to hold back, was that, yes, I *was* spoiled. For five years. Spoiled mercilessly. And then everything except my mom was lost. The house, the farm, and my father. Gone. When our dad died, Bill and Terry were already grown men. Both of them were married. Terry had a young son. Jen lived in Miami with her mother. Their grief—like their lives—was outside the farm, outside the state of Georgia, within their own families. When our dad died, I lost my whole world. But I was finding it again here with my brothers and sister. They returned me to the memories of the little girl I once was, the one who yanked off her clothes when she wanted, who let her hair grow long and wild, who ran feral and barefoot through the grass.

Bill came out on the terrace carrying a rum and Coke.

"Dad's favorite drink," he said, raising his glass in a toast.

He took the fourth chair, and we sat laughing and telling stories. I imagined what the barred owl high up in the oak branches saw, looking down at the four of us. The three of them are more closely linked physically, and there's more of my mother in my face than I realize. But we all have the wide Chester forehead, and our shared smile is unmistakably our dad's. There's something in our mannerisms too that points to kin. I thought of all the people I'd met along this journey, the friends and family that now formed a vast network running like thick roots just beneath the surface of my life. I looked around at my siblings and felt the strength in our connection. For the first time since I was a child, I knew I was held.

Terry was taking in this scene, too. "Dad had this fantasy, you know," he said, looking at each of us. "That one day we'd all move back to the farm in Georgia. We'd build our own houses nearby, and in the evenings we'd sit on the front porch in the rocking chairs and have a drink, all of us together."

Here we were, his legacy.

Acknowledgments

TO MILLICENT BENNETT, WHO HAD my heart at hello. An immensely gifted editor and the kind of woman I want to spend hours with talking books and bacalhau. How did we get so lucky?

To Anna Stein, the first person I trusted with this story, who told me ten years ago that it would be a book. I'll never forget that moment of faith in me and my work, or the many others like it along the way.

To the humbling number of people who contributed to this story. My profound appreciation for the newspaper articles and photos, the FOIA reports and court transcripts, the insights on aviation and criminal law. Thank you to everyone who talked to me about my dad.

About the Author

ARTIS HENDERSON's work has appeared in the *New York Times*, the *Daily Beast*, *Reader's Digest*, and *Sierra*, among others. Her first memoir, *Unremarried Widow*, was a *New York Times* Editors' Choice and named to more than ten Best of the Year lists. Artis has an undergraduate degree from the University of Pennsylvania, a graduate degree from the Columbia School of Journalism, and an MFA from the Program for Writers at Warren Wilson College. She is a Fulbright-National Geographic Award recipient. A certified master naturalist and advanced open water diver, she splits her time between Florida and Portugal.